PICK UP
Your Own
BRASS

RELATED POTOMAC TITLES

Bullets, Bombs, and Fast Talk: Twenty-five Years of FBI War Stories
—James Botting

On-Scene Commander: From Street Agent to Deputy Director of the FBI
—Weldon L. Kennedy

Ruse: Undercover with FBI Counterintelligence
—Robert Eringer

PICK UP
Your Own
BRASS

LEADERSHIP
THE FBI WAY

KATHLEEN MCCHESNEY
& WILLIAM GAVIN

FOREWORD BY TOM PETERS

Potomac Books
Washington, D.C.

Library of Congress Cataloging-in-Publication Data
McChesney, Kathleen, 1950–
  Pick up your own brass : leadership the FBI way / Kathleen McChesney and William Gavin. — 1st ed.
     p. cm.
  ISBN 978-1-59797-683-1 (pbk.)
  1. Leadership. I. Gavin, William. II. Title.

HD57.7.M39525 2011
658.4'092—dc22

2011004710

Printed in the United States of America on acid-free paper that meets the American National Standards Institute Z39-48 Standard.

Potomac Books
22841 Quicksilver Drive
Dulles, Virginia 20166

First Edition

10 9 8 7 6 5 4 3 2 1

CONTENTS

FOREWORD

It's been my secret—until now: writing forewords is all about ego. Mine. Of the literally hundreds of requests I've had, I've written no more than a half-dozen forewords. And each of those has been for a book that I considered to be of surpassing importance. Hence, I get to have the first word for something of remarkable value—which, in turn, makes me look good with the least bit of work.

First of all, what right have I got to be writing this? I'm a private sector guy, or so it seems. To begin with, I've put in (with pleasure) my public sector time—four-plus years in the Navy (Seabees in Vietnam, then the Pentagon) and two years more or less in the White House (staff director of the Cabinet Committee on International Narcotics Control). Second, there *are* universals. I get to "go out in public" because of a book I cowrote in 1982, *In Search of Excellence*. My coauthor, Bob Waterman, and I did indeed examine private sector companies, but our findings apply anywhere. The "excellent companies" were highly profitable, but the profit per se was not the goal. The profit was a derivative concept. That is, the profit came not from a love of money but from doing the right things right and being of service. While the book weighed in at over three hundred pages, I believe it can be summarized in four words: People, Customers, Action, Values.

That is:

- It all—100 percent—stems from remarkable people who are remarkably developed and remarkably led by true, ego-free servant leaders.

- We are all (FBI or McDonald's or Boeing) 100 percent in the business of providing extraordinary service to our clients (citizens or customers) 100 percent of the time.
- While thoughtfulness is imperative, nothing happens without an ingrained—some might say fanatic—100 percent "bias for action." ("A Bias for Action" was the first of our eight basic principles.)
- You are as good as your devotion to your core values. Let vigorous adherence to them slip to less than 100 percent and you lose the support of your constituents and members alike.

Each of these four governing ideas from *In Search of Excellence* is practiced within and could have been invented by the FBI. And these four ideas animate, with a clear passion, this book as well as my own.

You can (or should) fall in love with this book with no more than a glance at the chapter titles. They give away the plot. Here are a few that captured me in a flash: "Find the Best Talent"; "Leadership: A Privilege, Not a Right"; "Know Your People"; "Everyone Is the Face of Your Organization"; "We Can Do This!"; "The Action Imperative"; "It's Not About Me"; "Help! I Need Somebody"; "The Boss Is Not Always Right"; "Defend Your Team"; "Grandstands Are for the Circus"; "Saying Thanks"; "Not Everyone Is Going to Like You"; "Leaders of Leaders."

With the rest they add up to—from alpha to omega—the "right stuff" of inspired and effective leadership practice.

The book is extracted from the extraordinary experiences of extraordinary senior leaders, Kathleen McChesney and Bill Gavin, in an institution the great majority of us admire. Maybe some of us, the older among us at least, see the image of J. Edgar Hoover and a tommy gun when we think of the FBI, but for those of us who have had experience with the organization (I've had that experience, albeit only fleeting), the phrase that comes to mind is "thoroughly professional." There are, to be sure, high-publicity cases, but the real story is the hard, meticulous, overwhelmingly unglamorous, day-to-day work performed by thousands of committed agents and support staff members and a remarkable cadre of leaders who deliver the goods for three hundred million American citizen "clients" year in and year out. Making a case is not the front-page "perp walk," it's the mountains of "dull" and seamless detail accumulated over months and years that underpin solid indictments and eventual convictions "beyond reasonable doubt."

I have a core belief about management and leadership literature. A book may transmit ideas of extraordinary importance, but it is only as good as its stories! Here, once again *Pick Up Your Own Brass* stands out—way out. Not merely "cops and robbers" stories, these are stories of leaders and followers in the toughest and most complex circumstances imaginable, coming through time and again. (And screwing up too—you don't learn the ins and outs of leadership from wall-to-wall success stories!) Which is to say that for me, *Pick Up Your Own Brass* was indeed a "page-turner."

There are truckloads or trainloads of leadership books available. And I don't single out McChesney and Gavin's work lightly—hey, it's my reputation on the line, too. Among that small number of books I've written forewords for is *Reagan on Leadership* by Jim Strock. Well, the message of *Pick Up Your Own Brass* is in a league with the leadership lessons of our extraordinary fortieth president.

In short, writing this foreword has been an unalloyed pleasure and learning experience for me—as I'm sure reading the book will be for you. It's all about those basics of people and values and servant leadership—obvious in retrospect, honored in the breach all too often in the hurly-burly of daily practice.

Tom Peters
West Tinmouth, Vermont
November 23, 2010

PREFACE

For more than a hundred years, Americans have viewed the Federal Bureau of Investigation (FBI) as an agency of highly skilled investigators who protect civil rights and national security. FBI agents have been aptly described as badge-carrying, gun-toting law enforcement professionals who are led by men and women capable of managing complex investigations and directing dangerous raids and arrests. Many of the skills and qualities of the FBI's best leaders are quite similar to those of the best leaders in other organizations, but some are as unique as the agency itself. Beyond the skills and qualities of the most exemplary executives in any venue, however, lies a mind-set of ethical service and the strong belief in the privilege of leadership.

Since 1934 FBI agents have carried guns as a necessary tool of the trade. Extensive technical and legal training in the use of the Bureau's weaponry includes regular testing to guarantee that every agent, regardless of rank, is qualified to safely and accurately use the guns that he or she carries. During these testing sessions, agents fire hundreds of bullets, the casings of which are automatically or manually ejected from the firearms. At the conclusion of the tests, the casings—or brass, as they are called—are scattered about. Agents are then expected to clean up their shooting area by picking up their brass and disposing of it in large recycling barrels.

As part of their months-long initial training at the FBI Training Academy in Quantico, Virginia, newly hired agents attend firearms classes several times each week. Occasionally, a senior FBI official will observe one of these training sessions or may even decide to shoot along with the class. At the conclusion of the lessons, the young agents dutifully pick up their brass, and if their superiors are shooting with them, they gather their brass as well.

During a firearms training session for new agents some years ago, the instructor welcomed a visiting FBI executive to his class. The well-known and high-level leader humbly took his place at the end of the firing line and strictly obeyed the instructor's commands. When the class finished shooting, the official carefully reviewed his target. Seeming satisfied with the results, he bent down and picked up the brass that had been ejected from his weapon as well as that ejected from the weapons of the shooters nearest him.

At the next session, the trainees discussed range protocol with the instructor. One student remarked that he was surprised to see that the prominent visitor had cleaned up his own range area instead of allowing a subordinate to do that for him. The instructor, a former Marine Corps captain, smiled knowingly before making his point: "A good leader always picks up his or her own brass."

This high-level executive was entitled to have his subordinates pick up after him so that he could spend his valuable time attending to the important demands of his position. Nonetheless, by the simple act of picking up his own brass, he proved to the class that he was an equal; and by picking up the brass of others, he clearly demonstrated that he was a leader.

Whether you lead a team of law enforcement officers or an organization from Wall Street to Main Street, as the boss you will have unlimited opportunities to "pick up your own brass." Through simple, sincere actions, such as forgoing a perk or carrying your own bags, you can convey a high degree of respect for your subordinates, peers, stakeholders, and investors. More important, these types of efforts reinforce your employees' confidence and boost their morale, making it much easier for you and your organization to succeed.

• • •

We are grateful for the support of our agent, Jeremy Langford, of the Langford Literary Agency; our editors Don McKeon, Elizabeth Demers, Elizabeth Norris, Kathryn Owens, and Claire Noble of Potomac Books; and of every FBI agent we identify by name as an exemplary leader. We also thank our families and those friends and colleagues who read our work, helped us to recall events, and encouraged us to complete this project: Robert E.

Casey Jr., Philip Donegan, James Sheehan, Margaret Owens, James Ingram, James Botting, Weldon Kennedy, James B. Connolly, Anita Bajaioritis, Eileen Gavin, Jill Gannon, Jodi St. Ours, William Megary, David Grossman, Richard McChesney, and Louise McChesney. Any errors in this work are the regrettable result of imperfect memory.

INTRODUCTION

The FBI's century of service to America, and its investigative successes and achievements, have been the result of the collective effort, initiative, and dedication of thousands of employees. Subscribing to the tenets of fidelity, bravery, and integrity, loyal and enthusiastic FBI men and women have enabled the Bureau to develop and thrive through ten decades of war, espionage, organized crime, terrorism, fraud, and corruption.

There is no such thing as "just another day" at the Federal Bureau of Investigation. Hundreds of new and unique cases to investigate, pieces of information to analyze and disseminate, and bad guys to arrest are part of the FBI's daily rhythms. The value of the mission and the excitement that comes with carrying the FBI badge and credentials continue to attract law enforcement career seekers. Shifting security and intelligence priorities in the United States and the increasing volatility of criminals and terrorists around the world compel thousands of talented men and women to vie for the few coveted special agent positions that are available each year.

From its modest beginnings in 1908, the FBI has grown to become one of the most respected law enforcement agencies in the world. Over the years, many FBI leaders played a critical part in this expansion by providing the vision and the direction necessary to meet the Bureau's mandates of protecting the public and maintaining national security. When faced with changes in investigative priorities, such as unexpected crime problems, emerging criminal enterprises, or global terrorism, FBI executives have found ways to meet these daunting challenges with ingenuity and courage.

This book describes how many of the FBI's multitalented men and women led others—both formally and informally—with their energy, tenacity, and commitment, and it illustrates how exceptional executives improved the performance of those around them by their own actions and words. We also depict the actions and omissions of leaders that negatively impacted their subordinates or their work environments in order to provide a more complete picture of how people—even in a much admired institution—can be seriously mismanaged. To assist the reader in understanding the FBI and its hierarchical structure, we have included as an appendix a description of the FBI's leadership positions with a list of similar ones in the private sector.

From the examples in this book we have developed uncomplicated and sensible tips that can guide leaders and aspiring leaders in dealing with management challenges common to all types of organizations. FBI leaders we have admired inspired their peers and subordinates through their character and conduct. We hope that our messages help and inspire you to become a better leader for the benefit of others.

PART I

WHERE ARE THE LEADERS?

If an organization selects its leaders primarily from within, then it is incumbent upon the organization's administrators to recruit and retain employees interested in and capable of leading others. The rigorous process that the FBI uses to select special agents and other professional employees is perfectly suited to meet this objective.

Having the right talent in a potential leadership pool is only the first step toward maintaining a stellar leadership cadre. An organization—and the FBI is no different from others in this regard—must make its leadership positions attractive enough to encourage men and women to commit themselves to a career of dealing with issues, problems, and crises as they make the predictable personal sacrifices that all leaders must make.

Where the FBI is different from other organizations, however, is that its leaders perform roles that are critical to their country's safety and well-being. FBI leaders are financially compensated, of course, but not in the ways that business or nongovernmental agencies can reward exceptional performance. For FBI leaders, it is the privilege to lead that is the prize. Fortunately for all of us, talented, committed men and women step forward each day to earn that honor.

ONE

Find the Best Talent

Sheila Horan's radio alarm went off at 5:30 a.m. As usual, this was a chance to catch the important news of the day before heading off to work as the leader of the FBI's National Security Division at the Washington, D.C., field office. In her position as the special agent in charge (SAC), Sheila was a savvy, intelligent, and articulate twenty-two-year FBI veteran with many years of experience overseeing foreign counterintelligence cases. She was involved in nearly all of the FBI's most sensitive counterintelligence and counterterrorism cases. This particular sweltering summer morning there was an ominous report about two deadly bombings in East Africa. Sheila suspected that her responsibilities were about to change rapidly.

On the way to her office in northwest Washington, Sheila spoke by phone with Thomas Pickard, the assistant director of the Criminal Investigative Division at FBI Headquarters. Tom was handling matters for the FBI's second in command, Deputy Director Robert Bryant, who was out of town. He quickly updated Sheila on what he knew: two terrorist attacks—simultaneous bombings at the U.S. embassies in Kenya and Tanzania—had been confirmed. Unequaled in their ferocity, over 5,000 men and women had been injured, and, by week's end, 258 of them will have died in the attacks.

At the Washington field office, FBI agents and analysts had already begun to gather information about the devastating events. Their sources confirmed that twelve Americans perished in the violence, but most of the victims were from Nairobi or Dar es Salaam. Despite that difference, it was clear that the intended target of the mayhem was the United States. In order to find those

responsible and bring them to justice it would be necessary to deploy investigators, technicians, translators, and tactical personnel to Africa; to search
multiple crime scenes; to liaise with local law enforcement officials and the
U.S. Department of State; and to extensively interview witnesses and inform-
ers. And, not least of all, someone needed to be in charge "on the ground."

A few blocks away from Sheila's office, at FBI Headquarters, Director
Louis Freeh met with Tom Pickard and key counterterrorism officials. One of
the director's first priorities was to select and send an experienced leader to the
crime scenes. Without hesitation, he chose Sheila.

Seven hours and four inoculations later, Sheila was on her way to Nairobi.
Aboard a U.S. military-provided jet, Sheila and twenty FBI agents discussed
their investigative strategy and the likely suspects. A few wondered aloud about
the logistical challenges of working in another country, particularly one where
not everyone spoke English. They got to know the members of the Fair-
fax County, Virginia–based, renowned international urban search-and-rescue
squad, which was headed to Kenya with them to provide expertise in victim
rescue and recovery. While they talked and speculated about what lay ahead,
terrorism specialists in every FBI office around the world were reviewing intelligence records for clues that might lead to the identities of the perpetrators.

Eight long hours after leaving Andrews Air Force Base, the bare-bones air
transport landed at the U.S. naval station in Rota, Spain, for refueling. No one
was cleared to leave the plane as there had been too little time to obtain visas,
but most of the members of the group stood up and stretched their legs. A
few, including Sheila, looked out the windows as a diversion, hoping to catch
a glimpse of some interesting scenery on this short stopover. Within seconds
of smelling the slightest odor of something burning, Sheila turned away from
the window to look around the cabin. In the distance she saw small wafts of
smoke near the cockpit. Not waiting a moment longer, Sheila jumped from
her seat and immediately directed everyone to exit the plane. The passengers
quickly streamed out of the jet as the pilots called for help from the airfield.

Fire crews quickly arrived and extinguished an electrical fire that had created the smoke, but it was five more hours before the underlying problem
could be fixed. The tired team had already been awake for over twenty-four
hours and had another long flight ahead. Now, besides their fatigue, a few of

the men and women were beginning to have nasty reactions to the multiple vaccinations they had received hours before.

At 4:00 p.m. on August 8, 1997, a full day after the bombings, the plane finally reached its destination at the Nairobi Airport. Sheila, now running on adrenaline, grabbed her thirty-pounds of gear and headed for Immigration and Customs. Once there she was relieved to find the helpful State Department representative, who told Sheila that American and Kenyan officials were waiting for her at the FBI Command Post. Sheila and the representative guided the weary group onto a rickety city bus for the final leg of their journey. Clearly, there was to be no shower, no rest, and no meal in the foreseeable future.

During the next twenty-four hours, Sheila met with the courageous and compassionate U.S. ambassador Prudence Bushnell; the overwhelmed heads of the local police departments; the Canadian ambassador, who had graciously provided facilities for the FBI Command Post; and dozens of dismayed but dedicated embassy staffers. She prioritized key assignments for the members of the FBI's sleep-deprived team and made several calls to FBI Headquarters and to the FBI team leader in Dar es Salaam to provide updates on the investigation and request more personnel and supplies. Later, Sheila and Ambassador Bushnell met with the president of Kenya, Daniel arap Moi, and briefed him on the status of the investigation.

One critical issue was how to deal with the media. Ordinarily, in major cases of international scope, the FBI director represents the FBI. However, this was no ordinary case, and the need to share information with the world was urgent. Local citizens were apprehensive about their safety and wanted to be assured that a professional, well-staffed investigation was under way. Concerned Americans abroad were hoping to hear that these were isolated incidents and that the perpetrators had been apprehended. Foreign law enforcement and government officials also wondered if the same—or copycat—terrorists might target them too.

As the embassy's communications director made arrangements for the first of a series of press conferences with local authorities, Ambassador Bushnell told Sheila that she was expected to represent the FBI and the U.S. Department of Justice. Normally this would be the responsibility of the FBI director and the Bureau's professional spokespersons, but they were thousands of miles away. At that point, no one knew more about the scope and depth of the investigation than Sheila did. If she chose to contact FBI Headquarters for permission to speak publicly, it was possible that the Bureau's decision-making process could delay the press conference and impact the government's relationship with the media. Even more problematic was the possibility that she might be told to direct media questions to the officials at FBI Headquarters in Washington. Realizing how important it was to provide timely, reassuring information to the people of Kenya and Tanzania, Sheila decided to forgo asking for an approval from FBI Headquarters and joined Peter Mbuvi, the deputy director of the Nairobi police, in the press conference.

Sheila remained in Africa for the next five weeks to direct the FBI's investigation. Aided by an extensive network of investigators, contacts with intelligence officials worldwide, and the crucial support of the Kenyan and Tanzanian police, the FBI determined within days that the attacks were likely financed by the wealthy Islamic radical Osama bin Laden. Sheila was also the face of the FBI in Nairobi when President Bill Clinton authorized the military to launch cruise missiles into a terrorist training area in Afghanistan and ordered the destruction of a facility in Khartoum, Sudan, believed to produce nerve gas.

This unprecedented investigation extended well into 1999, and over nine hundred FBI investigators were ultimately deployed to key locations in Africa and the Middle East. The extensive efforts of the Bureau's federal and international partners led to the arrest and extradition to the United States of four members of the al Qaeda terrorist network involved in the bombings. On May 29, 2001, all of these men were sentenced to life in prison. Later, thirteen other suspects in this case, including Osama bin Laden, were placed on the FBI's Most Wanted Terrorists List.

During her time in Africa, Sheila saw the devastating personal impact of terrorism firsthand. As she was commanding the world's most important investigation, she was also ensuring that the growing number of FBI agents and specialists on scene had adequate personal safety equipment, food, shelter, and supplies. Because of her ability to quickly establish trusting relationships with law enforcement leaders, her constant concern for the welfare of the FBI employees, and her unlimited energy, Sheila Horan was the perfect choice to lead this incredible effort.

Clearly, not every FBI leader faces the challenges of handling an international terrorist attack. However, most possess the key qualities of a good leader. Through their actions, the best FBI leaders provide solid direction to the nation's most important investigations and support and mentor their subordinates and subsequent generations of leaders. Occasionally, a few fall short in their leadership roles because they fail to understand how to deal effectively with their coworkers or how to establish essential external partnerships. Sadly, others suffer from the inability to separate their oversize egos from their leadership responsibilities.

The FBI's hundred years of service to America and its organizational survival is not accidental. Since the Bureau's inception in 1908, through ten decades of war, espionage, organized crime, terrorism, fraud, and corruption, outstanding leaders like Sheila have held the agency together by providing the direction needed to strengthen and revise its mission, to refocus its resources, and to nurture its human capital. FBI leaders have been the driving force that models and sustains the tenets upheld by all special agents: fidelity, bravery, and integrity. It all begins with finding the best talent.

- Find independent-minded, mission-focused visionaries to build your organization.
- Select individuals of courage, integrity, and commitment to lead your organization.
- Choose leaders who understand and embrace their role in sustaining and improving your organization.

TWO

Leadership: A Privilege, Not a Right

Leaders come in all shapes and sizes, even in a buttoned-down organization like the FBI. Whether they are informal group leaders or they hold prestigious positions at the top of the agency, the men and women who represent the best of FBI leadership have both a keen understanding of the privilege of leadership and a strong desire to serve others.

Executives who believe they have a special right to be in charge miss the basic premise of leadership and generally fail to earn, or maintain, the respect of their coworkers. Those with top-notch management skills also struggle to be successful until they fully comprehend the responsibilities and opportunities of leadership.

As the executive assistant director for Law Enforcement Services, one of the FBI's highest-level positions, Kathleen McChesney was regularly involved in the selection of candidates for the Bureau's most prominent leadership positions. The personnel board that she chaired appointed entry- and mid-level managers, and she and Director Robert S. Mueller III frequently interviewed some of the more competitive candidates for top executive positions.

Most of the interviewees had never met the director before and were naturally nervous about making a good first impression and about answering his and Kathleen's questions intelligently. Some would hide their anxiety by trying to appear extremely confident or even humorous. The most open and honest candidates often began their interviews by admitting to how uncomfortable they were.

Once the word got around the Bureau as to how the director engaged the candidates, their responses and comments began to sound the same. Every now and then—and what made some of the discussions so fascinating—there would be a candidate like "Josh," who described his desire to be a leader in a brand-new way.

Josh was a very talented, articulate young man who had been a leader in another field before he joined the FBI. Already a top talent with a bright future, he had been promoted steadily through the FBI ranks. When it became evident that he was a competitive candidate for a senior-level executive position, Kathleen and Director Mueller interviewed him. The director knew what he was looking for in his key leaders—in particular, the qualities of strength, character, commitment, and aggressiveness. During his interview, Josh demonstrated those characteristics and impressed his interviewers with his unique work experiences, ability to communicate, and positive personal attitude.

As the interview was ending, the director asked Josh why he wanted to be promoted to a position of greater responsibility.

"Well, sir," Josh said with a handsome smile, "it's about the 'euphoria of leadership.'"

The director seemed to understand and appreciate the answer, but Kathleen wanted to hear more.

"Can you explain that for me?" she asked.

"Certainly," Josh replied. "It's that great feeling that you have when you are in charge of others. I experienced this feeling when I was in charge of a company of soldiers before I joined the FBI. I want this promotion so that I can experience this euphoria again."

Later, the director told Kathleen that Josh was the most impressive candidate that he had interviewed thus far in the FBI. "I like the guy," he said. "He's a go-getter, he's confident, and he's a leader. He is motivated to do well, he wants the position and, as far as the 'euphoria of leadership,' he seems to understand what it's all about."

It seemed to Kathleen, however, that Josh might be one of those managers who are more enamored with being the leader than in serving others. These types of officials—especially those solely motivated by the need for self-fulfillment—tend to be poor role models and often fail to provide adequate support or guidance to their subordinates. Nonetheless, the director seemed close to selecting Josh for the position. He asked Kathleen if she thought Josh really wanted this particular career opportunity.

"No, Director," she answered. "I believe that the job he wants is yours." Managers who fundamentally operate on the desire to be in charge often attempt to circumvent many of the necessary preparatory steps for leadership. They may be successful at "beating the system" for a time, but it is likely that their lack of relevant leadership experiences will deter them from achieving long-term success. Furthermore, ill-equipped supervisors who exhibit substandard performance lower the expectations of potential leaders who mistakenly begin to believe that they, too, have the capacity, and the right, to a leadership role. Fortunately, after Director Mueller selected Josh for a position with greater responsibility, he proved to be a very capable, committed leader focused on FBI goals rather than on personal aspirations.

- Regardless of the motivation for seeking a leadership role, one must recognize and appreciate that such a position is not a right but a unique privilege.
- The privilege of leadership creates unlimited opportunities to help employees succeed.
- A healthy, measured ego is an essential ingredient of leadership success.
- Holding a higher position in an organization is not the same as leading.
- Being the leader allows for the captivating and fulfilling experience of the "euphoria of service."

THREE

Ask Me to Lead!

One of the key strengths of the FBI is its rigorous selection standards for special agents. Many of the most sought-after qualities of a good agent—self-motivation, aggressiveness, and the ability to work well with others—are also the qualities of a good leader. FBI agents are generally second-career professionals, many having held supervisory positions in the military, business, or law enforcement. Consequently, the FBI has a perpetual and attractive pool of potential managers.

Drawing the FBI's most talented men and women to management positions is an increasing challenge. FBI leaders, like their private sector counterparts, look for top performers with the skills critical for meeting the organization's objectives and sustaining its reputation in the long term. Identifying these leaders is simple, but convincing them to take on greater responsibilities is not.

As fulfilling and exciting as being a leader in the FBI can be, some of the most gifted agents cannot be persuaded to take on the additional responsibilities of management. Institutional disincentives to promotion have plagued the FBI for decades. Moving up the FBI's ladder of success also means transfers, especially for those who are promoted beyond entry-level management positions. Those who reach the coveted special agent in charge (SAC) positions and head FBI field offices around the country have typically relocated their families several times.

These so-called career development moves come with an obvious array of hardships. The financial demands of buying and selling homes in various markets, the emotional issues children face in enrolling in a new school every few years, the impact on a spouse's career, and the time-consuming effort of finding new health care providers and community support can overwhelm even the strongest family. Those individuals who might be able to take these matters in stride must also understand that the additional compensation for increased responsibilities is minimal and capped by the federal government. The negative impact on salary and pension that is likely to result from a promotion forces them to carefully consider whether to "get on the train."

The pragmatic view of the FBI's Executive Development and Selection Program makes one wonder why agents endure these hardships in pursuit of a more impressive title and many more responsibilities. While FBI leaders have their own distinct stories, there is a commonality of purpose found among them. Like soldiers, these men and women are willing to make sacrifices for their country because they believe in the mission and in their ability to help the Bureau achieve its national security goals. They balance the pros and the cons of the impact of the FBI life on their families and volunteer to move ahead even when self-interest might suggest a different course.

FBI executive assistant director John Otto recognized that one of the most important things leaders can do for their organizations is to identify their replacements. In the Bureau, finding people with the ability and the dedication to develop organizational strategies, direct complex investigations, and command critical operations isn't difficult, but encouraging people to take on the many demands of law enforcement leadership is a formidable undertaking.

In the early 1980s the FBI was having a particularly difficult time attracting agents to supervisory positions owing, in large part, to the increased costs of relocation resulting from the nation's economic struggles. This smaller pool of available management candidates also created a reduction in the number of women and minorities interested in promotion. In order to deal with this problem and to establish a viable executive succession plan, John brought together FBI agents from all levels for a career development retreat. Kathleen was fortunate to be included in this meeting and had the opportunity to observe how the Bureau's most senior leaders solved difficult problems.

During this day-long meeting, there was no distinction in rank. All of the participants candidly told John what motivated or prevented them from taking part in management. Those who were already in positions of leadership described the disincentives of their roles, particularly the negative impact on family life that resulted from moving around the country. All those present agreed that the FBI had many highly qualified potential leaders and that the current challenge was to find ways to persuade them to become a part of the management cadre, even if it required some personal sacrifice on their part. John maintained that the most effective means of turning a bystander into a participant was to use the direct approach, that is, to simply ask a talented man or woman to volunteer for a leadership position. One of the senior executives in the room confirmed John's point. "Everyone likes to be asked," he said. "Whether they accept the challenge or not, it is important for people to know that others, especially their superiors, believe in their potential."

"We're not just here to listen to ourselves," John told the group. "We are going to do something to get more people into management." Speaking to the top-level leaders he said, "Let's get out to the field offices and meet with the agents. They need to know what leadership means to the FBI and to the future of this organization. If we can't get our talented people to step up to the plate, we have failed them, and, as its leaders, we have failed the FBI."

Always one to do what he asked others to do, John began to visit FBI field offices and meet with agents to talk about what it was like to serve the Bureau in a management position. While John and the other executives did not sugarcoat their roles in these informal mentoring sessions, they were able to generate interest and enthusiasm among the agents in building a better FBI. They succeeded in bringing in dozens of new leadership candidates who had been simply waiting to be asked.

- Without good leadership, an organization has no future—regardless of its size, mission, or resources.
- Key leaders have a responsibility to identify gifted and talented replacements for themselves and their colleagues.
- As leaders groom subordinates for roles of greater responsibility, it is important to remain sensitive to the personal needs of the emerging leader.
- Encourage, recruit, and retain the "best and brightest" through informal mentoring programs.

- Provide just compensation and family support if your company or agency's work necessitates executive relocation.
- Leaders can help the right people become great leaders by being the model they want others to strive to emulate.

PART II
LEADERS ARE EVERYWHERE

In the FBI, and in other organizations we have been associated with, there are many types and levels of leaders. Regardless of their place in an organizational hierarchy, each of these leaders contributes in a different, but essential, way to the manner in which the organization carries out its mission.

Some men and women carry a title that clearly classifies their role, such as supervisor or director, while others are "alpha leaders" who have no title that implies leadership but who lead their peers nonetheless. While they seldom receive the recognition that they deserve, the alpha leaders frequently use their natural leadership skills in pursuit of organizational objectives. Intentionally or not, they represent the organization through their words and actions much as the individuals who are its most highly ranked and visible leaders do.

In all organizations, true leaders share essential characteristics. They understand the people with whom they work and are able to identify goals and what is required to achieve them. They use their vision, optimism, and enthusiasm to motivate and energize their peers, and they are willing to take reasonable risks.

The best leaders, just as those described in the following eight chapters, can lead on the fly. They understand how much information is necessary to make a decision, and they will use their experience and, at times, the wise counsel of other leaders to determine how and when to take action. Just as important, the best leaders are patient when necessary and assertive when right.

FOUR

Know Your People

A New York City Police Department (NYPD) bus with all its lights flashing stood outside the Jacob Javits Federal Building in New York City. The bus and the motorcade of police cars and motorcycles behind it drew the attention of passersby on a chilly November afternoon. Inside the double glass doors of the office tower was a contingent of FBI agents wearing full Special Weapons and Tactics (SWAT) uniforms. The agents were equipped with the various weapons they typically carried as they headed out on a new mission.

On that particular fall day, Bill Gavin was meeting with Tom Sheer, the head of the FBI's New York office, to discuss an undercover operation. Tom's formal title was assistant director in charge, and as such, he was responsible for all of the operations and administration of this field office, the Bureau's largest. Before they finished their meeting, Tom asked Bill to go with him to the building's lobby, where the SWAT team was staging for an operation.

Tom had unique management skills and, even more important, tremendous leadership qualities. He was seldom caught off guard or flustered and maintained a casual but professional approach to everyone. This humble man never forgot that he started his productive and historic career as a "street agent," investigating cases, conducting surveillance, and arresting criminals. Perhaps that is why he was always available to talk with any employee, regardless of his or her position. If you hoped to learn how to be a leader, you merely had to stand back and watch Tom work.

The SWAT team was headed for Atlanta to assist in resolving a hostage situation at the federal penitentiary there. It was an experienced group, well prepared and regularly trained for dangerous situations like that one. To transport this special team to its waiting jet without delay, Tom had contacted his friend, NYPD commissioner Ray Kelly, who readily provided the escorts necessary to get the FBI team to the airport as soon as possible.

As the team lined up to board the bus for the airport, Tom reached out a hand and spoke directly with the first man in line. Calling him by name, Tom said, "Go to Atlanta, and make yourself and the FBI proud. And don't get hurt because you're the best we have!" As the agent moved on, he smiled broadly, his chest swelling with pride.

Standing behind Tom, Bill could hear him speak to the next agent in the same way, calling him by name and telling him, "You're the best we have!" As Tom repeated his message to every member of the team, anyone could tell from their faces that, despite the repetition, Tom sincerely meant what he was saying. After Tom spoke those inspirational words, it seemed that the men stood taller and walked away with both their resolve and their commitment strengthened.

Tom was truly concerned for the safety of the team during the next three weeks. The prisoners in Atlanta had taken over a three-story dormitory in their prison compound and were holding several hostages. Although he knew the on-scene commanders were providing strong leadership to the team and had even prepared a plan to retake the dormitory in the event that prisoners started to take the lives of the hostages, he hoped for a peaceful resolution. Fortunately, the hostage negotiators were able to convince the inmates to release the hostages, and the New York team returned home. Before they arrived, Tom made sure that he was at La Guardia Airport, where he was the first to welcome each team member home and to thank them for making the FBI proud.

Many in Tom's position would have remained in their offices while agents were sent off to a high-risk assignment. Instead, this leader was with the team members, offering each a word of encouragement and respect. As Bill watched these interactions, he could easily see that the respect was mutual. As an FBI leader, Tom was valued for his skills and admired for his sincerity. As a person, he was revered for his concern for his employees.

RECOGNIZE YOUR PEOPLE

Among Charlie Parsons's many unique talents is his nearly photographic memory for names, numbers, faces, and cards. As a skilled gambler he could visit nearly any blackjack table and come away a winner. This gaming expertise helped make him a highly successful organized crime squad supervisor in the FBI's Las Vegas office. When Charlie later became the head of the much larger Los Angeles office, he learned the names of its one thousand employees and regularly walked through the warren of squad bays to stop and talk with whoever was present. During his "walk-arounds," Charlie called each employee by name, mentioned their recent accomplishments, and thanked them for their efforts. If an employee brought a family member into the office for a tour and they ran into Charlie, he would use that occasion to again recognize the employee for his or her good work on a particular case or project.

Most of the best leaders we have known, whether in the FBI or another organization, are like Charlie and Tom. They understand the significance of knowing your coworkers' names and recognizing the importance of their jobs. Still, a small number of lesser leaders, including "Bernie," never caught on to the importance of conveying respect for others. Bernie always seemed uncomfortable with the casual, friendly manner of the employees on the West Coast. He preferred to conduct all of his work from his executive suite and tried to avoid contact with coworkers whenever possible.

Bernie faced a major logistical challenge in trying to keep to himself and to avoid interactions with his subordinates. To get to and from his office on one of the top floors of the federal building, Bernie had to endure a long elevator ride during which he was usually joined by several FBI employees. Bernie rarely acknowledged his coworkers in the elevator—on the contrary, he generally avoided eye contact with them. Whether he meant to or not, his demeanor transmitted a clear lack of regard for his subordinates, who would have appreciated even the slightest acknowledgment from the boss.

Once they figured out that Bernie wasn't going to begin to treat them with a modicum of respect, a few of the employees created an office game in which they deliberately tried to ride on the elevator with him. When they got into the elevator, some of the more daring employees would say and do outrageous things to get Bernie to speak to them. One fearless agent even went so far as to talk about Bernie to others in the elevator as Bernie stood silent and grim faced behind him.

Not surprisingly, Bernie's apparent disregard for the men and women in the office resulted in their low opinion of him as their leader. The employees accepted him as their authority figure and dutifully followed his instructions. In truth, they would have preferred to have a boss who was interested in them as individuals and who treated them with the respect they deserved.

- Know your coworkers' names and the roles they play in your organization.
- Reinforce your knowledge of your coworkers through frequent formal and informal dialogue with them.
- Show courtesy and sincere appreciation to coworkers by recognizing their accomplishments publicly and often.

FIVE

The Big Mirror

From the times of the earliest radio shows and gangster movies depicting the FBI as a well-honed, professional group of gun-carrying lawyers and accountants to the days of C-SPAN coverage of FBI executives testifying to Congress about budgets, operations, and plans, the public has been exposed to nearly every aspect of the organization. The FBI name generally conjures up positive responses and a high degree of approval from most Americans. Nonetheless, there are detractors and those whose opinions change from time to time depending on their experiences with, and observations of, FBI employees.

Journalists and news producers filter their impressions of the conduct and achievements of FBI agents in ways that can profoundly influence the public's opinion of the Bureau. There are many opportunities, however, for FBI men and women—regardless of their rank, title, or position—to represent the organization in ways that reflect its high standards and competency. Although all employees are well intentioned, some do better than others at generating confidence and admiration from those they meet—a skill that is expected of Bureau leaders.

Much has been made, and rightly so, of the warrantless surveillance program conducted by the National Security Agency (NSA) after September 11, 2001. The existence of the secret program, which was intended to identify individuals or groups planning to commit acts of terrorism against the United States, was confirmed by President George W. Bush in December 2005. This revelation, and the continued operation of this covert project, was of sufficient importance to cause both the House of Representatives and the Senate to investigate and hold hearings on the matter. Testimony from the FBI director and the former attorney general and deputy attorney general clarified many central, and a few extraneous, issues surrounding the surveillances and, at the same time, revealed some fascinating aspects of the characters of the government witnesses.

According to their recorded congressional testimony in 2007, Attorney General John D. Ashcroft Jr.; his deputy, James B. Comey; and FBI director Robert S. Mueller III had serious concerns about the program. Some of their concerns had been addressed and modifications made, but without additional changes the attorney general would not approve the surveillances beyond March 10, 2004.

Notwithstanding Attorney General Ashcroft's objections to the program, White House general counsel Alberto R. Gonzales was desperate for the Justice Department's approval. As the deadline approached, Mr. Ashcroft became ill with pancreatitis and was hospitalized. Owing to the severity of his illness, he delegated his powers to Mr. Comey, who had already indicated to the White House that he would not provide the requested approval on behalf of his superior or the Department of Justice.

On the evening of March 10, 2004, instead of seeking out Mr. Comey, who was unlikely to help them, Counsel Gonzales and White House chief of staff Andrew H. Card went to visit Mr. Ashcroft in the hospital. Forewarned by a telephone call from the White House, Mr. Ashcroft's chief of staff contacted Mr. Comey about the impending visit.

Mr. Comey rushed to the attorney general's bedside to prevent the two men from the White House from taking advantage of his ailing boss. On the way, he called Director Mueller to let him know what was occurring. Director Mueller instructed the FBI security detail to see to it that Deputy Attorney General Comey remained with the attorney general during the expected visit.

When Mr. Gonzales and Mr. Card entered the attorney general's hospital room and explained that the purpose of the visit was to seek his approval for the NSA program, Mr. Comey knew that he had been right to be concerned. As Mr. Comey later testified before Congress, Mr. Ashcroft, as ill as he was, lifted his head from the pillow, reiterated his objections to the program, and then lay back down.

"I was angry," Mr. Comey testified. "I thought I had just witnessed an effort to take advantage of a very sick man who did not have the powers of the attorney general because they had been transferred to me."

Mr. Gonzales and Mr. Card left the hospital before FBI director Mueller arrived, although Mr. Mueller was then briefed on the substance of the meeting by Mr. Comey and Mr. Ashcroft. Interestingly, Mr. Gonzales later told members of the House Judiciary Committee that the conversation at Ashcroft's bedside did not involve the NSA program. By this time, Mr. Gonzales had replaced John Ashcroft as attorney general of the United States.

In their subsequent testimony before members of Congress, both Mr. Comey and Director Mueller refuted Mr. Gonzales's characterization of the nature of the hospital meeting. Their assertions were grave and to the point: Mr. Gonzales and Mr. Card had in fact asked the ailing attorney general to approve the surveillance project that night. Given the fact that Director Mueller was then working directly for Mr. Gonzales and Mr. Comey had worked for Mr. Gonzales before leaving the Department of Justice, they came to be greatly admired for their candor and courage in dealing with this grave issue.

A more stunning revelation in their testimony, however, dealt with the possibility of resignations. Both Director Mueller and Mr. Comey confirmed that they and former attorney general Ashcroft had been prepared to resign from the government if the warrantless surveillance program were to continue without the changes that they believed were necessary to make it a legal program. The fact that three of the highest-ranking federal law enforcement officials in the United States had considered such a drastic step to protect the rights of citizens was historic and, unsurprisingly, bold.

Anyone who knows Director Mueller or Deputy Attorney General Comey is well aware that they do not bluff, prevaricate, or become entrenched in political gamesmanship. Director Mueller's forthright words to Congress exemplified the integrity and independence that FBI employees expect and demand from their leaders. His admirable leadership actions and the quality and nature of his testimony will forever reflect favorably on the FBI.

- The top leader of an organization is its single, most important public face.

- The power of a leader's actions and words is directly related to the quality of his or her character.
- The impact of a leader's most notable actions and words reflect on everyone in the organization.
- In difficult situations, a leader must do what is right—and take notes.

SIX

Everyone Is the Face of Your Organization

Individuals can do things so amazing and laudable that their actions make their associates, and even their entire organization, seem stellar. Likewise, one employee can do enormous damage to an organization by an unprofessional, unethical, immoral, or illegal comment or act. In either circumstance, the actions of one person can taint all the others.

Every FBI agent, regardless of assignment or rank, is expected to be a leader, part of a team of leaders, or a leader of leaders. FBI agents, as leaders, have two special responsibilities in this regard. First, they have to make certain that their employees know that each of them represents their organization and every member thereof to the public. Second, they must recognize that everything that they do and say, from the most inconsequential remark to the most impressive act of bravery, will be evaluated and scrutinized by others. It is a rare, perfect leader who will make no public mistakes. The rest of us must be diligent and honestly introspective about our words and actions so that they will reflect well on our fellow employees, and the organizations, we serve.

"Owen" was somewhat atypical for an FBI agent. Although intelligent, well educated, and hardworking, he had few friends in the office. His social skills seemed to be underdeveloped, and he often made inappropriate, though not rude, remarks, especially to women. As a result, Owen's supervisors tried to give him assignments requiring limited public interaction, especially with business or community leaders.

By chance, the SAC of Owen's office met a very successful businesswoman who was intrigued by the FBI. After discussing the similarities in their professions, the businesswoman mentioned that she had recently been interviewed by an FBI agent and had been highly impressed by his demeanor. She described the agent as polite, professional, and articulate and thought the FBI was lucky to have him as an employee.

The SAC was surprised when the woman identified Owen as this remarkable agent. Everything the woman had said about Owen was extremely complimentary, and she wanted his boss to know that her confidence in the FBI had been bolstered by meeting Owen. Though Owen was in an entry-level position, his unexpected and positive actions with this influential citizen had reflected especially well on the SAC as well as on Owen's hundreds of colleagues.

PROBLEMS AMONG PARTNERS

Neil Gallagher was the head of the FBI's Counter-Terrorism and Counter-Intelligence Division at FBI Headquarters when he learned that a conflict had developed between the FBI and two other major law enforcement agencies. At the time of the dispute, Neil knew an immediate solution was required and that one or more high-level visits to the key officials of the other agencies was necessary. Unavailable to handle the matter himself, Neil reached out to Kathleen McChesney, the SAC of the FBI's Chicago office. Neil and Kathleen had worked together before, helping agents develop and conduct undercover operations aimed at preventing terrorist acts. He thought she would be able to resolve the issue and reestablish the cordial relationships that once existed between the FBI and these important partners.

The problem that generated Neil's call involved a sensitive FBI investigation targeting suspects of significant importance to the other two agencies. Although aware of their interest, agents assigned to FBI Headquarters had conducted a covert operation against these suspects without notifying the other agencies. The good news was that their efforts were extremely successful, and the agents were able to gather critical evidence for their case. The bad news, and what impacted negatively upon the relationships, was that the information should have been brought to the attention of both agencies quickly, but it wasn't. The officials were certain to be angry with the FBI about the agents' failure to properly notify them of their activities.

Kathleen asked Neil what he wanted her to do.

"I need you to go and see all of the officials. Apologize. Lots of times. And by the way, can you go tomorrow?" he said.

Kathleen spent the next four days in repair mode. She visited with the top leaders of each agency and briefed them on everything that had occurred. More important, she apologized for the agents' mistakes. She suggested solutions that might help to repair the relationships among the agencies while the FBI continued to gather evidence that would benefit everyone's cases.

As expected, all of the parties were incensed. By the end of the first round of meetings, however, most, although not all, of the men and women agreed to move forward in a civil fashion. Nonetheless, it was apparent that it would take some time to reestablish the valuable relationships that had once existed.

Kathleen visited the partners twice more as the operation continued, expressing continued regrets for the poor judgment of other FBI agents. Fortunately, the humbling mea culpas began the rebuilding of two of the FBI's most key interagency partnerships and led to the development of dozens of other important shared investigations.

WHEN HUMOR ISN'T FUNNY

Occasionally, and perhaps accidentally, the FBI promotes a man or a woman whose speech is more entertaining than substantive. These types of individuals are generally fun to be around, and they can usually be relied on to amuse an audience with a quip or an observation. They can also be painfully irreverent and cause irreparable harm to the target of their joke and to the reputation of other FBI leaders.

One such witty executive, "Art," traveled from his senior position at FBI Headquarters to a large city to speak to an important gathering of law enforcement leaders. He began his talk with a series of one-liners targeting the largest police department in the area as well as its chief. Seemingly oblivious to the fact that the crowd wasn't laughing, Art went on for several minutes as the other FBI personnel in the room began to get angry with him. There was a very real possibility that Art's comments would lead the police officers, with whom the FBI agents worked every day, to believe that their FBI counterparts had a low regard for them when, in fact, their relationships were solid and productive.

At another event Art introduced his boss to a conference of government attorneys by first denigrating the attorneys in the room and then by mocking his own leader. Once again, the FBI employees who were listening to him were shocked and mortified. Although his peers sometimes secretly hoped that this executive would get his comeuppance, it never happened. Surprisingly, his boss, a man with a fairly serious demeanor, tolerated Art's court jester personality, leaving many to wonder why.

- An employee's words and actions can create a lasting public impression of your organization and its people.
- Ensure all of the members of your organization understand their special responsibility to represent one another in a positive, professional way.
- Be prepared to take responsibility for the errors of your colleagues.
- The ability of leaders to represent an organization can be accomplished through training and example.
- Provide corrective counsel to employees who fail to present themselves in a positive, professional manner.

SEVEN

That's Why You Hired Me

For many years the FBI special agent recruiting model was fairly unsophisticated and decentralized. The head of each field office usually appointed an agent to attend the occasional college or high school career fair and fill out the necessary paperwork for new hires. The strength of the FBI brand attracted thousands of highly qualified candidates each year; therefore, it seemed unnecessary to make any significant changes in the way the Bureau identified and selected its new investigators.

Not long after he became FBI director, William H. Webster recognized that the agent population was a collection of very talented and experienced men and women that lacked substantial racial and gender diversity. In addition, only a small percentage of the on-board agents had the special scientific, engineering, and language skills needed for the Bureau's increasingly complex, global investigations.

Most college graduates do not aspire to a law enforcement career, but Director Webster believed that the FBI could do more to attract different types of people to the agency, especially those who more closely reflected the general composition of American society. Clyde Groover, the FBI's assistant director for administration, agreed with Director Webster on this point and established the FBI's first national hiring program to meet Director Webster's goals. With the right leadership and a more coordinated recruiting approach, Groover was convinced that the new initiative would increase the Bureau's outreach to a wider variety of candidates.

Doug Rhoads was a well-known agent assigned to the FBI's satellite office in Charlottesville, Virginia, who immediately impressed those he met with his ability to communicate effectively with individuals at all levels in the Bureau. During his many years in the FBI, he had established a reputation as a superb investigator, affable colleague, and confident public speaker. This former decorated army officer was a natural leader among his peers and an enthusiastic representative of the organization. When Groover selected Doug for the new position of national applicant recruiter, those who knew Doug were certain that he was the right person for this unique job.

Once Doug moved to Washington to take the position, it was clear that it was a perfect fit for him. As he had been in the military, Doug was committed to public service and understood the importance of a highly capable and values-driven workforce. He viewed this assignment as an opportunity to be as creative as possible and, at the same time, to make a significant impact on the future of the FBI.

Although Groover had not made any specific promises about how the new office would be funded and staffed, Doug naively believed that he would have the same type of administrative support and financial resources as other entry-level managers in the FBI who were responsible for conducting or overseeing investigations. To Doug's surprise, when he arrived at FBI Headquarters, he found an empty office, a telephone, and a new boss who was preoccupied with hundreds of other personnel issues.

Undeterred and perhaps even more challenged to move ahead, Doug identified a number of actions that needed to be taken if the agency was to establish a legacy recruitment program. During their first meeting, Doug's busy boss intimated that he would be distracted from more urgent matters if he had to review and approve every one of Doug's initiatives. Rather than become frustrated by the thought of having to pick and choose which actions needed to be brought to the boss's attention, Doug interpreted his boss's remarks as tacit approval for him to do whatever was necessary to get the program moving.

As a low-level manager, Doug had limited decision-making authority, and yet he knew that many of the initiatives he wanted to implement probably required the authorization of his Bureau bosses. To that end he creatively found different ways to make many of his projects appear to have the approval and backing of his superiors, never failing to interject the director's desire to hire a more diverse workforce into his presentations and memorandums. Doug's aggressive approach convinced others to help him implement his program. Once they were successfully in place, he publicly attributed the great results to his bosses, who had not been involved at the outset but who accepted the accolades nonetheless.

Doug's leadership philosophy and "leading-from-the-bottom" style drove the immediate success of the recruiting program. He prioritized his tasks and developed a long-term recruiting plan to replace the budget-driven hiring model that the FBI had used for decades. He convinced the FBI director that the SACs of the field offices were to be responsible for recruiting quality personnel in their territories and should be held accountable for their efforts—or lack thereof. At first this was seen as yet another way for FBI Headquarters to add another administrative responsibility to the SAC's job description, but the SACs came to realize that Doug was right in engaging FBI leaders in this worthwhile new project in order to foster its success.

As a result of Doug's vision and the efforts of the small staff that he developed, the FBI's recruiting program improved significantly. In the span of three years, the number of women and minorities hired as special agents doubled. Recruiters were more carefully selected and consistently trained by human resource professionals, and every new special agent applicant benefited from the more streamlined and efficient hiring procedures.

The self-confidence born of experience that such leaders as Doug possess enables them to accurately evaluate the next steps in the context of what is best for a particular endeavor, an organization, or its people. Although Doug wisely kept his bosses apprised of his progress, he initiated many actions that could not wait for approvals from multiple layers of FBI managers. Others may have considered his boldness inappropriate and, perhaps, career defeating, but Doug correctly believed that taking the right action, at the right moment, was imperative.

I HAVE AN IDEA

Special Agent in Charge Joe Jamieson of the Philadelphia field office knew how to conduct a proper street surveillance. He had conducted many stakeouts and tailed more than his share of bad guys in his career. He also understood that, despite their possible creativity, clean-cut, white, middle-aged men driving nondescript, dark-colored, four-door sedans faced enormous challenges when trying to follow criminals and spies in some environments.

The difficulties in conducting a successful surveillance were made worse by the fact that most sophisticated targets were always on alert for the "Feds on their tail" and would employ all kinds of tactics to evade the FBI. When one of Jamieson's squads developed an especially important case involving two KGB spies, he became determined to find a way to put more distance between the agents and the people they would be watching so that they would not be "made" by their targets.

Hoping to augment the surveillance teams with additional observers and to enable them to watch their targets from greater, more discreet distances, Jamieson believed it was essential that the FBI use light aircraft. In 1966, however, the FBI did not own any aircraft; previous recommendations made to FBI Headquarters to include an airplane in budget requests to Congress had fallen on deaf ears. Furthermore, using airplanes was not an approved FBI surveillance technique; consequently, there were no arrangements to lease airplanes from local owners.

Regardless of his inability to get Bureau support for using aircraft, Jamieson decided that the importance of the case at hand outweighed the potential negative outcome of his violating the FBI policy. Jamieson didn't know how to rent, much less fly an airplane, so he sought out the assistance of one of the young agents assigned to the office, Oliver B. "Buck" Revell. Jamieson knew that Buck had been an aviator during his service in the Marine Corps and figured that he knew a great deal about aircraft. When Buck told Jamieson that his pilot's license was current and that he had multiple ratings, Jamieson knew he had picked the right person to help him test out his theory.

Later that day, Buck and Jamieson drove to a nearby airfield and located a four-seat Cessna 150 that seemed suitable for air surveillance. At Jamieson's direction, Buck used his government-issued gasoline credit card to rent the plane so as to avoid too much scrutiny into their activities from FBI Headquarters. With Jamieson and others on the ground acting as suspects, Buck flew the Cessna on a trial run that confirmed the technique would work in an urban environment. A second test flight with a transmitter and antenna on board using exclusive Bureau frequencies proved that the pilot and the ground teams could communicate at distances up to sixty miles.

When it came time to finally follow the suspected spies, everything worked perfectly. As Jamieson had expected, having an "eye in the sky" allowed the agents following the suspects to maintain a safe distance from their targets. From the aircraft, Buck could guide the agents around the streets in such a way that they would not lose track of, or be detected by, the people they were watching. From this surveillance, the agents ultimately proved that the KGB had two active spies in the United States working without diplomatic cover. Soon, other squads began to ask Buck to fly surveillance for them so that they, too, could more effectively and discreetly watch the suspects involved in their cases.

Jamieson made certain that Buck was reimbursed for the airplane rentals and finally admitted to his superiors at FBI Headquarters that he had been violating the Bureau's policy against using or renting aircraft. But open minds prevailed, and this extraordinary technique became routine in Philadelphia and many other FBI offices.

As time went on, the bills for the airplanes started to add up. Other issues, such as maintaining the confidentiality of the rental and insurance details, and the availability of equipment needed to be addressed. Jamieson was promoted and transferred to Los Angeles, where the consistently good weather allowed agent-pilots to fly airplanes nearly every day. He was convinced, more than ever, that the time was right for establishing a national aircraft program for the Bureau.

Optimistically, Jamieson began to campaign for new assets. Buck, now a supervisor at FBI Headquarters, also strongly advocated this project with the expectation that the use of airplanes would ultimately benefit the entire organization in a variety of ways. Ironically, Jamieson and Buck had taken risks to use aircraft contrary to FBI policy and now found themselves in positions of influence where they could openly campaign for the planes.

A few years later Congress approved the purchase of several used aircraft, and the FBI's official aircraft program was inaugurated. Jamieson's persistence, Buck's persuasive skills, and the success of their surveillances had ultimately convinced the decision makers of the importance and urgency of this initiative. Later, when Buck was the assistant director of the FBI's Criminal Investigative

Division, Director William Webster put him in charge of the entire Aviation Program. Buck was finally able to place aircraft and qualified pilots in every FBI office and secure special-purpose aircraft to support the rapid response of the Hostage Rescue Team agents, technicians, and photographers to critical incidents.

Today the FBI has a sophisticated surveillance system that provides critical investigative support. The development of the Bureau's Aviation Program is an obvious testament to Jamieson and Buck's vision and determination to do what is necessary to get the job done. It is also a vivid example of how results-oriented leaders can improve a functional process and enable their organization to more effectively meet its goals and achieve its mission.

- Regardless of the importance of a project, without the support of the right leader, it will not develop quickly, if at all.
- The perception of leadership support of a project can be just as effective as active support.
- Achieving the appearance that superiors are behind your project requires the confidence that it will succeed.
- It is sometimes easier to apologize for failing to seek permission to take an unprecedented action than to waste time obtaining permission.

EIGHT

We Can Do This!

One of the most important issues being discussed at FBI Headquarters when Burdena "Birdie" Pasenelli arrived in 1993 to become the assistant director in charge of the of the Finance Division was the condition of the FBI's laboratory. Since 1972, the laboratory had been housed on several floors of FBI Headquarters at Ninth Street and Pennsylvania Avenue, NW. Over two decades later, the facilities were woefully inadequate for the volume and types of forensic analyses the FBI conducted for its own cases and for a large number of other law enforcement agencies from around the world. Though the laboratory had set the benchmark for many of the internationally recognized standards of forensic science application and research, it could not realistically expand its analytical capabilities without more room for equipment, storage, and research.

Several FBI laboratory directors had attempted to improve its infrastructure by creating a "state-of-the-science" facility. The FBI made repeated budget requests for approval and funding of a capital project for a new or remodeled laboratory only to be denied by external reviewers. Scientists and laboratory aides worked in cramped and crowded quarters, and if any new employees were hired, they had to share precious exam space. The longtime assistant director of the laboratory, John Hicks, and his successor, Milton Ahlerich, were also concerned about the increasing number of requests for examinations and the FBI's ability to complete scientific tests in time for court hearings.

Birdie knew the capabilities of the laboratory well and its importance in solving cases. As an FBI agent, and before that as a Seattle police officer, she had made frequent requests of laboratory examiners to review evidence she had collected. Many times these exams had produced a key clue that led to the identification of a suspect or the conviction of a defendant. Birdie was worried that the FBI's reputation as a leader in the field of forensic science might now be diminished if the laboratory could not keep pace with new scientific developments such as the identification of suspects using DNA analysis.

As the discussion and dreams about a new laboratory continued, some employees at FBI Headquarters grew concerned about working in a building that co-housed traditional office space with a large, busy laboratory. One day the supervisor of the payroll office called Birdie about a foul smell permeating the office space in the basement where dozens of employees processed the FBI's biweekly paychecks and employee expenses. The offensive odor in their area was making it very difficult to work.

Birdie immediately visited the payroll offices and saw that a drainpipe from the FBI laboratory ran through them. It was definitely the source of the stench, and, as Birdie soon learned, this was not the first time the air in their offices had been tainted. A new laboratory was clearly overdue. A veritable optimist, Birdie was confident that she could find a way to acquire the funding to build a new laboratory outside FBI Headquarters. She promised the employees that she would get it done.

The procedures for developing large projects in the FBI are similar to those in the private sector or a nonprofit organization. An individual or group with a vision makes a business case for an idea, takes ownership of its development, and follows it through to completion. The project "owner" has to have a keen understanding of the economic and political realities of the distribution of organizational resources if he or she hopes to be successful. For project owners in federal agencies in particular, the value of having friendly supporters in the Office of Management and Budget (OMB) and Congress when you look for new capital cannot be overstated. Although Birdie was the very busy head of the FBI's Finance Division, she also became the project owner for the new laboratory once she committed to the FBI director and the laboratory employees her belief that, collectively, they could make this idea a reality.

Remodeling FBI Headquarters to accommodate the laboratory's growth was not a viable solution, so Birdie began a campaign to locate land and secure funding for an entirely new building. Her first success came when suitable property was acquired from the Marine Corps on its base in Quantico, Virginia, next to the FBI Training Academy. As it turned out, this was a relatively easy task compared to the challenge of convincing Congress to appropriate money for construction.

On April 19, 1995, domestic terrorists bombed the Alfred P. Murrah Federal Building in Oklahoma City, causing the deaths of 168 men, women, and children. The FBI was responsible for conducting the investigation of this unprecedented loss of life and quickly used up most of the financial resources intended to support FBI counterterrorism investigations throughout the year. To remain solvent in this area, the FBI prepared a supplemental counterterrorism budget request that needed to be approved by both the Department of Justice and Congress.

Before the request for supplemental funding was submitted, however, Birdie realized that a unique opportunity to obtain the initial funding for construction of a new laboratory existed at that particular moment. The FBI laboratory was integrally involved in the complex terrorism investigation in Oklahoma, and its examiners had identified the serial number on the rental truck that had carried the bomb and ultimately led to the identification of Timothy McVeigh as the bomber. Furthermore, FBI scientists were now inundated with thousands of pieces of evidence from the crime scene to evaluate. The overwhelming forensic work associated with this single case had pushed the laboratory facility beyond its limit.

Support for major capital projects is not always universal in organizations, and the FBI is no different. Robert "Bear" Bryant, the assistant director of the Intelligence Division responsible for the oversight of the Oklahoma City bombing investigation, did not support funding this project through a supplemental counterterrorism funding request. Although Bear and Birdie were close friends and equally dedicated to providing the best possible support for the FBI and its law enforcement partners, Bear thought it inappropriate to cite this tragedy as part of the justification for a new FBI laboratory. Director Louis Freeh listened to both of their perspectives and wisely decided to include the laboratory construction as part of his supplemental funding request to Congress.

After months of working on her adopted issue with her motivated budget and laboratory teams and garnering support from the Department of Justice's budget office and congressional staffers, Birdie successfully made her business case for the new laboratory and start-up funding. When Congress approved the FBI's supplemental counterterrorism budget request that included $25 million for the laboratory, it marked the beginning of an exciting multiyear construction project—the largest in the FBI's history. The new laboratory would provide first-rate work space for its five hundred employees. The plans also included scientific classrooms for the many specialized training courses that the FBI presents to crime lab examiners from around the world and sufficient space for expansion.

Birdie's vision of the laboratory and her confidence that the FBI would obtain the approval and funding for the project allowed her to develop and implement a highly successful strategy. The results of Birdie's efforts are clearly evident when one visits the new FBI laboratory. This operational, research, and educational center will skillfully support the global law enforcement community for years to come. For those who know of the countless challenges faced in reaching this goal, the new laboratory serves as a striking example of one woman's leadership, foresight, and optimism, as well as the enthusiasm and commitment of the hundreds of FBI employees who journeyed with her.

- Leaders often assume responsibility for important projects that are not their own.
- Visionary leaders illuminate what is possible for their employees and their organizations.
- Goal-oriented leaders understand that it takes plans, actions, faith, and a loyal team to achieve success.

NINE

Leadership on the Fly

Several years ago, Special Agents Hadley McCann and Ken Thompson teamed up to work with veteran Special Agent Sam Williams to conduct an investigation of organized crime and corruption connected to dozens of suspects and their businesses in Oakland, California. Their investigation had direct connections to ongoing cases in Chicago and New York and was rapidly becoming one of the largest in the country. Dozens of FBI agents from San Francisco and Oakland were assigned to assist Hadley, Ken, and Sam in gathering evidence that would be used to convince a federal grand jury to indict their targets for racketeering.

After several months of work, these lead agents were certain that they had identified the key players in the conspiracy and had gathered enough evidence to bring charges against them. Despite the wealth of information they had amassed, they realized that photographs or audio recordings of the suspects planning their crimes would be more convincing to a jury than the testimony of eyewitnesses or even a paper trail. The subjects of this case were not the responsible, honest businessmen they appeared to be in public, and the team had to find convincing ways to demonstrate their true character.

Investigative techniques, such as covertly recording conversations of suspects or videotaping them in private locations, can only be utilized if they are preapproved by a designated federal or state judge. To obtain such approval, agents are required to prepare affidavits, or sworn statements, for the court describing the basis of their investigation, the steps they have taken to find

proof of the crime or conspiracy, and the reason that conventional investigative methods are not likely to be successful. This is a time-consuming and
arduous process but well worth the effort, because audio and video recordings
can save time and expense for investigators. More important, these types of
exhibits help jurors to understand better the intentions of the defendants and
the elements of the crime.

Hadley, Ken, Sam, and their new partner, Special Agent Glen Breedlove,
were determined to do all that they could to make their case. They applied to
the federal court in San Francisco for an order to electronically intercept, listen
to, and record the conversations of their suspects, fully expecting to overhear
discussions that would confirm key aspects of the racketeering conspiracy and
reveal information about related felonies.

Court order in hand, the agents were eager to get started. They committed themselves to a ninety-day work schedule with no days off in order to be
able to follow all pertinent leads and to meet all of the reporting requirements
established by law and by the judge. Hadley and Sam scheduled agents to
listen to and summarize conversations from the wiretaps and to conduct briefings for other agents working on the case. At the same time, Ken coordinated
the investigation with agents from other FBI offices to solidify the criminal
connections between the suspects in different cities and to gain a better understanding of this network of con men and thieves.

Even the best investigations can experience setbacks and distractions, and
this case was no different. An important witness was found dead before he
could testify in front of the grand jury, a major earthquake rocked the San
Francisco Bay area and damaged some of the agents' homes, and one night
Sam was injured when a man who had just robbed a fast food outlet in downtown San Francisco shot him. Nevertheless, the case progressed, propelled by
the enthusiasm and optimism of its leaders.

One afternoon during the wiretap phase of the investigation, Ken received
a telephone call from an excited agent in another FBI office. The agent relayed
information from an informant that a key suspect in Ken's case was about to
head to a secret meeting with an important business figure. Ken gathered a
group of agents and quickly established a plan to locate and follow the suspect. This ad hoc surveillance team sped to the warehouse where the suspect
was supposed to be waiting for a ride to the meeting. When they arrived, the

agents were unable to find the suspect, but, relying only on Ken's thirdhand information, they decided to wait for him to show up.

As the hours passed, Ken grew mildly anxious about the information he had received from someone else's informant. Nonetheless, the details the informant provided about the suspect seemed to coincide with some cryptic conversations recently overheard on the wiretap. If the meeting occurred, it could lead to the identification of a new, high-level target—just the kind of lucky break an investigator hopes to get.

Ken got on the radio and rallied his bored and tired troops. The agents clearly wanted action and results, and Ken, with his positive attitude and high spirits, was able to motivate them to stick it out a while longer by stressing the importance of this opportunity.

Two hours later the suspect finally emerged from the warehouse, looking quickly but carefully around the street to see who might be watching for him. Within seconds a black sedan (of course) pulled up to the curb, and the suspect jumped in the front passenger seat. Instantly the surveillance team was reengaged and followed the car to downtown Oakland, where the driver parked outside of a bar. The suspect got out of the car and entered the bar, followed by two agents from the surveillance team. Inside the bar the agents observed the suspect meet with a well-known businessman, thus confirming that a relationship existed between the two men. By eavesdropping on their conversation throughout the evening, the agents were also able to gather new information about planned criminal activity. Ken's natural optimism, supported by his investigative experience and intuition, had now resulted in bringing an important aspect of this case to a higher level.

The following Saturday night, two fairly new and inexperienced agents reported for their midnight shift of wiretap duty and found Hadley talking with an FBI technician. Apparently something had gone wrong earlier in the day with the wire connections used to tap into the suspects' phone lines. No one had been able to overhear a conversation for more than twelve hours. Hadley had come in from home to try to help the technician fix the problem, and he worried about how many important calls had been missed.

As the agents waited for the phones to be reconnected, they read newspapers and caught up on reports on their own cases. They speculated about the technician's abilities and whether Hadley might decide to give up on the operation that evening. To his credit, Hadley had not lost his patience over the problem or the amount of time it was taking to fix the wiring problem that had already impacted his case and caused him to lose investigative ground. He also knew that the technician would rather be at home with his family than struggling with this problem in their dingy undercover office. Finally, the technician discovered an external problem. He reached someone at the telephone company who promised to make the necessary line repairs immediately.

Hadley was delighted to know that the fix was imminent. Nonetheless, he also realized that he had to spend more time with two perturbed agents, whom he barely knew, as they cooled their heels waiting to get to work. After a few awkward, quiet minutes, it occurred to Hadley that this unscheduled work time might actually be an opportunity to provide some informal training to these investigative neophytes and get them refocused on the case. Hadley invited them into the supervisor's office and explained the evolution of this case and its importance to the FBI's organized crime program. He discussed the advantages and disadvantages of dealing with criminal informants who occasionally provide dubious information to law enforcement officers in hopes of receiving some type of plea bargain or other personal benefit.

More important, Hadley talked to these new agents about why he believed this case was going to be successful and about the many actions it would take to make that happen. By the end of the midnight shift, the telephones were working again, and the agents had a far better understanding of racketeering investigations and FBI operations and were enthusiastic about the small part they were able to play in this large case. They had witnessed a leader's patience and hopefulness turn a discouraging evening into a chance to educate and to mentor.

Ken and Hadley had the ability to recognize opportunities that needed to be pursued as well as those obstacles that were too difficult to overcome. Their hopeful outlooks generated commitment and loyalty among the other agents, whose contributions were essential to their investigation. Their confident, combined leadership approach brightened the spirits of the other agents and caused their entire team to focus on their wins rather than on their losses.

- A team of optimistic leaders enhances a project and increases its chances of success.

- Good leaders will seize every opportunity to teach their craft to their subordinates.
- It is vital to maintain patience when circumstances are beyond your control.

TEN

The Action Imperative

Kidnapping cases present FBI agents some of their greatest investigative challenges. The gravity of the circumstances tests the leader as well, forcing him or her to make life-and-death decisions. Notwithstanding the time pressure and inherent difficulties in trying to recover a victim safely and arrest the kidnappers, the professional rewards of a successful case are remarkable.

Agents who are assigned to investigate kidnapping cases generally also investigate other types of dangerous crimes, such as bank robberies and extortions. These types of fast-breaking cases can stretch personnel resources thin, especially if several occur at the same time. During a very unusual week in the spring of 1995, there were seven unrelated kidnappings in the Los Angeles area. It was Ron Iden's responsibility, as the head of the office's violent crimes and drug investigations branch, to oversee the investigations and to make critical decisions about arrests and raids.

One of these kidnapping investigations began when "Lourdes," a woman from a Seattle suburb, called the local police to report that her husband "Tito" had possibly been kidnapped by some of his cousin's "business associates." When he went missing, Tito had been working for his cousin, "David," for several months by picking up and delivering "merchandise" in the Los Angeles area.

Police officials in Tito's hometown contacted Ron in Los Angeles and requested assistance from the FBI in locating Tito and David, who was, unsurprisingly, a prolific drug dealer with an extensive criminal record. Ron assigned several agents to find out what they could about the two men. Another group of agents set out for David's likely hangouts, while a third team attempted to find and interview his associates.

As the agents were following their leads, Lourdes received a telephone call from Tito. He told her that he had, in fact, been kidnapped, but before he could tell her more, one of the kidnappers took the phone from him. The kidnapper told Lourdes that David owed him $10,000 and that he intended to get that money before he would release Tito.

Tito's wife was frantic. Although she had a phone number for Tito's cousin, she had not been able to reach him and was unable to pay the $10,000 ransom herself. Fortunately, her telephone conversation with the kidnapper was long enough for Ron's team to employ new technology to determine the general location in central Los Angeles where the call originated.

The kidnappers had made several other calls to Lourdes, and the agents were able to determine that the calls were coming from a particular community known for its large population of gang members. Ron sent surveillance teams into the neighborhood to look for suspicious activity, as technicians further narrowed the source of the calls to a one-block area.

Ron carefully reviewed the notes and sketches from the surveillance. Something wasn't adding up. The buildings where the calls were suspected to be originating were "quiet." None of the surveillance agents had noticed any peculiar activity outside them that might indicate someone was being held inside against his will. Puzzled, Ron drove past the buildings and looked around for himself. The neighborhood was a run-down mixture of small, single-family houses and an occasional lackluster business.

Ron's observations were similar to those of the surveillance teams. In fact, the house with the strongest telephone signal appeared to be occupied by a family with young children going about a normal routine. Ron circled the block and came back for another look. On this second drive-by, Ron saw what seemed to be a separate residence in the rear of the property that was attached to the main house by at least one wall. During those brief moments, Ron also noticed a man standing near the back residence. The man looked around quickly, as if to see if anyone was watching him, and then went inside.

Time is usually of the essence in a kidnapping case. Neither David nor Tito had surfaced, and the kidnappers' calls to Lourdes were becoming more demanding. Based on what he saw and the telephone signals, Ron felt certain that Tito was being held in the rear residence. He ordered the SWAT team to attempt a hostage rescue.

With a search warrant in hand, two dozen members of the SWAT team entered the front and rear residences simultaneously. In the rear residence, which turned out to be a makeshift one-room apartment added on to the original structure, the team found several men and cell phones. To the surprise of some, but not to Ron, Tito was found as well, unhurt but bound with ropes and duct tape and secreted behind a tall chest of drawers. Ron's investigative experience and skill had led him to gather enough information to make a critical decision about when to take action. Others, such as the FBI official in the following situation, can become dangerously wedded to the belief that taking action is imperative in every circumstance.

THE BEST VIEW IS AT THE SCENE

FBI agents were having a difficult time identifying the members of a particularly violent gang of bank robbers active in several western states because they were always completely disguised when they entered the banks and were careful not to leave any items behind. On occasion a self-interested gang member might provide information to law enforcement that helps to solve such cases, but in this case no one was coming forward. Offers of rewards for information were unsuccessful. The agents were becoming increasingly frustrated as the thieves hit bank after bank, carrying automatic weapons and using notes that threatened to blow up the banks if their demands for cash were not met.

After several months without leads, an alert citizen who had heard about the string of robberies saw some men who were acting suspiciously in a car near a bank. Thinking that the men could be criminals, he noted the car's license plate number and turned it over to the FBI. The license plate number was registered to a car occasionally driven by a man who had a criminal record for robbery and assault, and this information provided the first, and most vital, lead in the case. Dozens of agents then fanned out over several states, trying to locate the car and its owner.

When the suspect was finally located, he was living in an old log cabin in a remote wooded area. The cabin itself was located at the end of a long road off a main highway and was closely surrounded by trees and brush, making it very difficult to stake out. No one had yet come forward to provide inside informa-tion about the suspects or any members of the gang, so in order to identify all the players, agents planned to follow everyone traveling to or from the house.

At 3:00 a.m. on the fourth day of their surveillance, the team saw the first signs of activity when lights went on in the house. A short time later, a mud-splattered white utility van and a silver-colored SUV pulled away from the house, heading for the highway. A challenging surveillance ensued with FBI agents having to follow at fairly long distances to avoid detection. The van and SUV traveled north together for nearly two hundred miles before stopping at a highway rest area. Several men got out of the two vehicles to talk and use the facilities. An undercover agent also stopped at the rest area and got out of his car to get a better look at the men.

As the surveillance was taking place, the SAC and the SWAT team com-mander from the nearest FBI office were overseeing the events from their command post. Coincidentally, the office was testing new technology that en-abled executives at FBI Headquarters to monitor and communicate via radio with the field office command post and the agents on the surveillance. The gang's activities had captured the interest of several high-level FBI officials, and they were listening closely to the activities taking place thousands of miles away.

After several minutes the men took off again in their van and SUV. But instead of continuing north, they turned around and headed south. Forty-five minutes later, they pulled into a typical suburban strip mall occupied by a doughnut shop, a tanning salon, and a small bank. The van parked near the front of the bank, where employees were preparing to open the doors for the day, and the SUV parked several hundred feet away on a side street. An agent in the command post who knew the bank manager called him and said that there was a strong chance that a robbery was about to occur. He suggested that the manager close the bank. The manager quickly posted a note on the bank's door indicating that the bank would be closed for the day and discreet-ly directed the bank employees to move to the rear of the bank.

At 10:00 a.m., customers started arriving at the bank's front door only to find the Closed sign. After several customers walked away, one of the men in the van jumped out and went to read the sign for himself. Within seconds, he was back in the van. It pulled out of the parking lot and headed toward the interstate. The SUV hurriedly departed as well, followed at some distance by the FBI agents.

Apparently hungry after their long journey, the suspects next stopped at a very busy café frequented by truckers and traveling families. Two agents, posing as a couple of road-weary travelers in search of a hot meal, went into the restaurant after the suspects. The agents quietly communicated back to the command post what they saw—a very crowded, confined business filled with dozens of people having a late breakfast. Sitting in an unmarked car in the busy parking lot, another agent reported that it had begun to rain quite hard, making it difficult to see or move quickly.

Suddenly, one of the officials at FBI Headquarters directed the agents over the new, experimental radio link to arrest the men at the restaurant. The test of the new radio system had been successful in terms of being able to clearly communicate over long distances but had thrown an unnecessary distraction into the operation. Orders for arrests in cases like this are made by the on-scene commander, such as the SAC, and not by headquarters officials. Furthermore, the suspects were very likely to be armed and possibly have explosives and automatic weapons in their vehicles. It was clearly not the right time for this action.

Amazed at the audacity of the official who had barked out the order, the SAC immediately countermanded it. It was apparent that the official had been overcome by the "action imperative," because to arrest five dangerous men using only a half-dozen FBI agents and no police backup in such a congested location was not only unnecessary but foolhardy. At that point, the SAC disabled the extraneous radio link to FBI Headquarters.

After the suspects finished eating and returned to their vehicles, the surveillance continued. They drove south, possibly to return to the cabin. By the time both of their vehicles stopped for gas, enough agents had gathered to be able to surprise and safely arrest all of the suspects. Agents found dozens of automatic rifles and handguns and several explosives in the van and SUV, along with maps and notes pertaining to various unsolved bank robberies. Clearly these violent criminals needed to be stopped, and the patience and clear thinking of the agents and their leaders on the scene had led to that desired result.

In this case, the SAC and the headquarters official agreed that there was a need for law enforcement action, but the SAC was convinced that in order to protect the bystanders and the agents and successfully capture the suspects, action was not imperative at the moment they entered the crowded eatery. The headquarters official, perhaps caught up in the unanticipated moment of being able to listen to the unfolding events, felt strongly that action had to be taken simply because the suspects were in sight.

• • •

Whether an organization's mission is to manufacture a product or to protect the public, its leaders need to know how to gather and process information that will enable them to make intelligent, proactive decisions. Even the most experienced and talented leaders will make errors in judgment and perhaps proceed in ways that are unnecessary or even harmful. Leaders occasionally mistakenly believe they will be perceived as weak if they do not act at every given opportunity.

Leadership development is considered a luxury in some organizations. It takes time that could be used to conduct business, generate revenue, or perform expected services. Nonetheless, relevant and meaningful training that provides leaders and potential leaders with the opportunity to learn from the experiences of others and to exercise decision-making and direction skills without fear of disastrous result or public criticism is essential to an organization's success.

- There are times to take action and there are times to wait. Even the wisest leaders will not always recognize the difference.
- Allow subordinates to learn decision-making skills through their personal experiences and your good example.
- Be mindful of false pressures that may influence you to act when intuition suggests otherwise.

ELEVEN

Taking Risks

The utmost care and caution in the decision-making process does not always result in a flawless outcome, but the leader who fails to act when necessary will certainly not succeed. Thousands of times each day, FBI leaders make decisions that involve some degree of risk. The experienced executive who has common sense, intelligence, and courage is able to accurately weigh the risks against the objective and then implement an appropriate course of action. There are times, of course, when despite a leader's best intentions, the decisions are imperfect and the results disappointing. As an FBI leader, Bill Gavin was keenly aware that if his decisions resulted in an unfavorable outcome, he must accept the consequences and learn from them.

Some years ago a group of Jamaican cocaine dealers living in southern Florida came close to destroying their community by conducting their illegal business with impunity from their homes, cars, and especially out on the streets. When they couldn't smuggle in enough of their product, they would steal cocaine from their competitors. They protected their enterprise through violence—by murdering those who owed them money or, worse, by torturing or killing the family members of their adversaries.

The group had dominated the illicit drug trade in the area for many months before one of their associates became so fearful for his life that he approached the FBI. This anxious insider believed at this point that only a law enforcement response could prevent the gang from killing more people. Working with the information the informant provided, a resourceful squad of

FBI agents began to formulate a plan to neutralize this group and end its reign of terror. The squad members and the leader of the SWAT team knew that an operation of this type would be extremely dangerous. The safety and security of the public were paramount as the agents created a plausible scenario that would bring the Jamaican gang to justice.

The drug dealers conducted their business in secret, protected locations, making it difficult to catch any of them performing specific illegal acts. Furthermore, they also used cocaine themselves and were often high and paranoid, making them more unpredictable. The agents agreed that providing something of value to the group—in this case an easy way to steal cocaine—would be the best way to lure them out into the open. They developed a detailed plan to covertly provide information to the suspects about a large quantity of high-quality cocaine in the area that was stored in such a way that it could be easily stolen. FBI agents and police officers would watch the storage area, and when the suspects came to steal the cocaine, they would be arrested after the theft occurred.

This plan required Bill's personal approval as the special agent in charge of the office. Some SACs, having little experience in conducting narcotics investigations, were reluctant to approve operations that had any element of risk. Other leaders recognized that aggressive, but prudent, actions were necessary to effectively deal with volatile drug gangs, and Bill hoped that he fell into this category. In this case, it seemed that the opportunity to capture these criminals, even with the possibility of a violent response, was an assumable risk that must be taken. To permit the continued killing and abuse of innocent people was not an acceptable alternative.

Based on their history of violence with firearms, the suspects who came to the prearranged location would likely be armed. There was also a chance that some members of the group would attempt to take the drugs by force or violently resist arrest. In light of these dangers and the possibility that a gunfight could erupt, the plan was refined. Bill directed the team to rehearse it to identify potential difficulties in its execution.

After the run-through, Bill ordered more changes in the plan to further guarantee the safety of the law enforcement personnel and their ability to gather evidence for the underlying investigation. He made certain that the

agents and officers understood the reasons for the changes and fully appreciated the difficulty of their task. Finally, when he felt that the plan was insightful,
purposeful, and as carefully calculated as possible, he approved the operation.

Given what his subordinates were facing, Bill knew there was some risk of
injury. But everyone was tactically trained and committed to doing what could
be done to destroy the grip of terror that this gang had on the community. As
their leader, Bill also knew that he would shoulder the responsibility should
anything go wrong. Even with the most careful arrangements in place, high-
risk situations can turn violent quickly. Still, he felt comfortable that the agents
would act in accordance with the plan they had devised and rehearsed.

On the night of the operation, Bill was at the scene, careful not to interfere
with the execution of the plan but ready to provide leadership and support as
needed. As darkness set in around 7:00 p.m., four of the gang members arrived at the prearranged location—a storage facility in an industrial district
with few lights and only one street leading in and out. The drug dealers were
clearly expecting to take what they believed was multiple kilograms of cocaine,
but within minutes they realized that they had walked into a law enforcement
setup. They responded with firepower aimed directly at the agents and the
officers. In the firefight that ensued, two of the Jamaican gang members were
killed and the other two were wounded.

Regardless of who is killed or injured, deaths or injuries resulting from a
law enforcement action are tragic. Nonetheless, Bill remained confident in his
decision to proceed, and he dealt with both the positive and negative consequences of the events that took place. Careful preparation had brought down
a dangerous group and surely saved many lives from being lost to a continuing
drug war. He was justifiably proud of the way in which the agents and other
law enforcement officers dismantled this violent gang.

As in other law enforcement agencies, FBI protocol mandates an internal
inquiry whenever weapons are fired during an arrest. In this case, the inquiry
conducted by the inspectors from FBI Headquarters was extensive. Though
tedious, these examinations are important in determining if the leader has
properly planned for the safety of the employees and the public in potentially
hazardous situations. Each SAC is required to justify his or her plans and actions to the inspectors and is inevitably subject to some second-guessing by
peers and superiors. As Bill expected, this operation, and the decisions made,

were found to be thorough, conscientious, and well executed. This was a case in which the risks had clearly been worth taking.

- Realistically identify and evaluate as many risks as possible before making critical decisions.
- Make certain that the elements for success are in place when executing your plans.
- An internal review of significant planning and decision-making processes may reveal important, previously overlooked facts.
- Encourage an external post-action review of any high-risk decisions and plans.
- Accept the consequences of your decisions, learn from them, and share those lessons with peers and subordinates.

PART III

PEOPLE MATTER

The importance of collaboration in successfully achieving a goal is obvious. One leader, or a team of leaders, committed to working effectively with others can bring a group of people together and accomplish a great deal. Meanwhile, if one self-important leader demands to be in charge, success will be much more difficult to achieve. Every leader is responsible for demonstrating collegiality and respect for his or her coworkers and external partners and maintaining the key relationships necessary to meet the mission. Above all, it is the people that matter.

Occasionally the lines of interpersonal relationships in the workplace are murky, but it is paramount for the leader to be concerned about the personal and professional well-being of his or her employees. Although it can entail a substantial amount of time, employees who are troubled or are in trouble need their leader's special attention. A leader can and should do what he or she can to help a subordinate overcome a problem and remain a productive team member.

Every organization has standards—whether formal or informal—that outline the core values by which its business is conducted. Employees are expected to uphold those standards. If they fail because of a false sense of entitlement or personal character flaw, it falls to their supervisors to address the misconduct and its consequences. An organization that ignores employee transgressions will damage its value system and, quite likely, its reputation as well. Leaders have a special responsibility, therefore, to protect the institution while ensuring that employees accused of wrongdoing are investigated fairly and with appropriate empathy.

One of the worst things a leader can do is to be an impediment to his or her employees and hinder their efforts by micromanagement or lack of support. Although some men and women work very well without any interaction, oversight, or guidance from their superiors, most people require and appreciate the interest and respect of a boss. Key to this interest and respect is the leader's ability to communicate effectively. Despite a leader's good intentions, at times his or her words can be misinterpreted and cause anxiety or harm to their employees or colleagues. Nonetheless, good leaders will use their communication skills to motivate and inspire their people.

TWELVE

It's Not About Me

FBI agents had been investigating federal crimes for nearly seventy-five years before they joined the Drug Enforcement Administration (DEA) and state and local law enforcement agencies in tackling the enormous problem of illegal narcotics entering the United States and the extensive, international money laundering associated with the smuggling. For reasons that were never quite clear, Director J. Edgar Hoover had been adamant that FBI agents leave the investigation of drug cases to other agencies. Ironically, the FBI had successfully investigated organized crime families that were also involved in drug trafficking and had frequently used techniques such as wiretapping that could be very effective against drug cartels.

In the early 1980s there were many drug investigations being conducted by individual law enforcement agencies throughout the United States. The agencies' leaders quickly recognized the inefficiencies and the potential safety risks associated with these overlapping investigations. The importance of sharing information, resources, and technology about the drug crimes and criminals was becoming more critical each day and had captured the attention of many public officials.

To compel law enforcement agencies to work together productively and with clearly defined priorities, Congress passed legislation creating the Organized Crime and Drug Enforcement Task Forces (OCDETF) in 1982 and the High Intensity Drug Trafficking Area (HIDTA) program in 1988. Though structured and funded differently, OCDETF and HIDTA were the sandboxes to play in if a law enforcement agency wanted to receive any of the generous federal funding that had been appropriated to fight the war on drugs.

Many major cities in the United States were designated by the National Office of Drug Control Policy as HIDTA locations, including Los Angeles. This particular distinction confirmed the enormity of the illegal narcotics problem in Southern California and the need for a collaborative, coordinated approach to investigations. As important, it allowed the Los Angeles law enforcement community to benefit from additional federal antidrug monies.

Under the HIDTA umbrella, law enforcement leaders in Los Angeles agreed to organize the specific tasks associated with drug investigations and assign them to distinct, mission-focused, multiagency groups known commonly as task forces. Various law enforcement agencies provided the officers, agents, or analysts who composed the task forces. The leadership responsibilities for each entity were divided among the member agencies and departments so that no single agency or department controlled all of the functions.

Of the many operations that came about as a result of these arrangements, one of the most valuable and enduring was the Los Angeles area Joint Drug Intelligence Group (LAJDIG). The LAJDIG's mission was to furnish useful analytical products to the investigative components of the Los Angeles HIDTA. These materials were synthesized from information provided by officers, detectives, and agents about individuals or groups who were smuggling or selling narcotics and laundering their proceeds through local or international businesses.

After a reasonable period of development, Charlie Parsons, the SAC of the Los Angeles FBI office, and his partners on the LAJDIG Executive Board recognized that the LAJDIG had yet to meet its full potential as an information-gathering and intelligence-sharing operation. During its initial phase of operation, the LAJDIG staff had created a policy and procedures manual and established a structure that would maximize the talents of the participants from the various federal, state, and local law enforcement agencies, but they weren't moving along as quickly as had been envisioned.

When the concept of the LAJDIG was approved by the leaders of the Los Angeles area law enforcement agencies, it was decided that an FBI supervisor would be in charge of the daily operations as director, with at least one assistant director assigned from a state law enforcement agency. Now, as Charlie wanted the LAJDIG moved to a higher level of operations, he suspected that a different management approach might be in order.

Charlie had been impressed with Don Johnson, an FBI supervisor responsible for investigating violent gangs in south-central Los Angeles and thought he might be the right person to lead the LAJDIG. Don's team was working very effectively in partnership with Los Angeles Police Department (LAPD) detectives and officers by using innovative techniques to gather evidence against the gang members. More important, Don had been able to capitalize on the distinct skills and experiences of the police officers and the agents in a complementary and highly effective way.

When Charlie told Don he was transferring him to head the LAJDIG, Don saw a compelling challenge ahead. He recognized the enormous potential for LAJDIG to help the greater law enforcement community. He also knew that the LAJDIG was one of the larger multiagency projects in the country and that he would have to encourage the member police departments and federal agencies to send capable, enthusiastic men and women to be a part of this initiative.

Don had previously been a part of the FBI's liaison team with the White House and the Department of State and knew full well the importance of cooperation and civility. Although Don was now in charge of the LAJDIG, he thought it critical that he share his leadership role with the assistant director from the local law enforcement agency in order for the group to achieve maximum success. Before he packed up his FBI memorabilia from his office in West Los Angeles to move to the LAJDIG facility, Don contacted Kim Markuson, a lieutenant from the Orange County Sheriff's Office who was assigned as the second in command at the LAJDIG.

To Kim's surprise, Don asked him to share the top LAJDIG leadership role with him. Kim had been assigned to the LAJDIG since its inception and had helped to establish the framework for operations. Kim was enthusiastic about the possibilities for the LAJDIG and readily recognized the positive impact having coleaders from two very different law enforcement organizations would have on the LAJDIG members and the staff.

"There is no 'I' in TEAM," Don explained. "If this group is going to work, we need the total cooperation of everyone. As coleaders, we will show the member agencies that we can cooperate, collaborate, and get things done. And another thing—we're going to have fun doing this, too!"

For this venture to do well, both men realized they had to be true partners. Kim appreciated and accepted Don's offer to be codirector, and from that day forward they jointly supervised the LAJDIG. When this new leadership team addressed the LAJDIG employees for the first time, the officers, agents, and analysts were an eager but disjointed group of representatives from a dozen different agencies. A few were cynical about the group's potential for providing useful intelligence to the HIDTA, and some were apprehensive about working for an FBI supervisor or a police lieutenant—or both!

Don put the folks at ease with his easygoing manner. "Park your badges at the door," he said. "We—all of you, Kim, and I—are going to move things forward and do great things at this JDIG. We will make a difference for all of our agencies, but all of you have to help."

Having two leaders can destroy the concept of unity of command, but for Kim, Don, and the LAJDIG, this was the right strategy for the time. Before their initial meeting was over, this team of leaders had reenergized the employees, established priorities, and created better policies for protecting information and informants. The investigators and analysts began to generate new ideas for constructing and sharing their research "products" and proudly developed the motto "LAJDIG: Gather, Analyze, Protect, and Share."

Don and Kim further demonstrated their commitment and cooperation by meeting with the head of every law enforcement agency and the commander of every drug task force and squad in the region to listen to their respective needs and expectations of the LAJDIG. They brought the observations and requests back to the team and solicited input on how best to serve its client members. Through many roundtable discussions with their employees, they found ways to address key issues and showcase best practices.

As the LAJDIG expanded, the two leaders maintained the "badge-blind" policy, treating all of the staff members the same, regardless of their rank or agency. They consistently recognized the team's individual and collective achievements. These leadership actions helped to build a camaraderie within the group that enhanced the work environment and strengthened relationships among all the participating agencies.

The LAJDIG continues to be a highly successful intelligence group providing invaluable support to the law enforcement agencies in Southern California. The intelligence generated by the group flows daily to law enforcement officers and detectives, helping them to piece together the puzzles of drug cartel businesses and organizations. The work of the LAJDIG also helps to "de-conflict" potential crossover situations, in which different law enforcement groups are unknowingly investigating the same suspects.

So effective is LAJDIG's leadership and operational model that it has been replicated by another group, the Los Angeles Joint Regional Intelligence Center (LAJRIC). The LAJRIC provides comprehensive intelligence services to law enforcement agencies throughout California and is itself an example of successful collaboration. By focusing on the goal and coming together as a team, both the LAJDIG and the LAJRIC showcase the best efforts, and the best results, of cooperative law enforcement.

PLAYING WELL WITH OTHERS KEEPS THE SANDBOX ORDERLY

One leader, or a team of leaders, committed to working collaboratively with other leaders can bring a group together and accomplish a great deal. Conversely, if one leader demands to be totally in charge, success will be much more difficult to achieve. On occasion, an FBI leader has unrealistically estimated his or her self-importance and exhibited an institutional arrogance that has been detrimental to a shared mission and ultimately diminished the FBI's reputation among its fellow agencies. It is more often the case, however, that FBI leaders respond ably to the critical need to "play well with others," especially where the safety and security of Americans are at stake. By demonstrating respect for their law enforcement counterparts and by demanding the same behavior of their coworkers, these leaders build and maintain the key relationships necessary to protect all citizens in this ever-changing and more inter-connected world.

Volatile inmates in a federal prison created a dangerous situation that no warden ever wants to occur on his or her watch when more than hundred inmates took nine employees hostage at the Talladega Federal Correctional Institution in Alabama. These desperate prisoners, many of whom were violent criminals awaiting deportation to their native Cuba, were willing to take dramatic actions to have their demands met. This started a chain of events that drew the attention of the nation for days and tested experienced law enforcement leaders from several agencies, including the FBI.

The Bureau of Prisons (BOP) is responsible for the safety and security of its institutions, but the FBI has investigative jurisdiction over crimes committed in federal correctional institutions. As events unfolded in Alabama, it became clear that the BOP would need operational as well as investigative support from the FBI. At the time of the incident, Bill Gavin was serving as the SAC of the FBI's very busy Miami office. That fact, however, did not deter FBI deputy director Floyd Clarke from asking him to travel to Talladega to assist Alan Whitaker, the head of the FBI's Birmingham office, along with fellow SACs William Baugh and Wayne Gilbert.

Four federal prison wardens and BOP executive Kathleen Hawk Sawyer had already been dispatched to Talladega to deal with the situation. The sandbox in which this group of leaders found themselves was chaotic for the first forty-eight hours. Notwithstanding their eagerness to provide assistance to their BOP counterparts, the FBI personnel recognized that the arrival of executives from other agencies can sometimes be more hindrance than help. Furthermore, the potential for conflict between agencies in a highly charged atmosphere is real. Major disagreements, particularly public ones, can be detrimental to the resolution of a crisis.

The collective goal was simple: to resolve the incident safely and restore calm to the institution. Nonetheless, the possible ways to bring about that peace were complex. Everyone knew that they had to quickly work through their differences and egos before they could be assured of any sort of successful outcome. Bill sensed some discomfort on the part of the BOP officials and acknowledged their concern that outsiders intended to take control of a situation in a facility that BOP clearly knew and understood far better than the FBI ever could. Once the BOP officials were reassured that the FBI's objective was to work with them—by relying on their expertise and experience and by supplementing efforts with the unique talents of the FBI employees—the ad hoc leadership team was able to act.

This group immediately established command teams, made up of a BOP warden and an FBI SAC, for each shift. This decision proved very effective in demonstrating solidarity and fostering communication between and within the two agencies. By merging all BOP and FBI personnel for the purposes of negotiating with the prisoners and conducting any tactical operations, the leaders created, in effect, a single and purposeful operational entity. This was much easier said than done, however.

The first meeting between the joint commanders of the BOP's Special Operations Response Team (SORT) and the FBI's Hostage Rescue Team (HRT) was critical. The tension between the teams was palpable and the body language cold, but everyone listened intently as the team leaders described their special skills. The SORT had essential knowledge about the prison's configuration and special inmate-handling procedures and was experienced in facing down similar encounters, whereas the HRT had unique, well-tested covert techniques for specialized electronic surveillance and other resources that would make any operation safer. Once the two teams became familiar with each other's capabilities, the anxiety level diminished on both sides. Information was openly exchanged, and critical operational alliances established. The FBI executives acknowledged the professionalism of all of the team members, appropriately discarding their misconceptions of the BOP's tactical team. The two teams finally became one, and everyone focused on the common mission.

The next few frustrating days were spent attempting to resolve the situation through dialogue with the hostage takers. As the discussions continued between the FBI hostage negotiators and key prisoners, the SORT and HRT members made contingency plans for a hostage rescue and developed a range of strategies. From their careful planning, it was clear that both teams understood the dangers of independent operations and would not attempt to take any actions on their own.

After eight days of intense negotiations, everyone was rightly concerned that a negotiated settlement with this disjointed band of prisoners was unlikely to occur. When the prisoners who were acting as representatives for the inmates were overheard discussing their plans to murder one of the hostages, the joint leadership group agreed that a tactical resolution was required. The command team, which now included Acting U.S. Attorney General William Barr, who was ultimately in charge, approved a plan that combined the element of surprise with the best tactical capabilities and resources available.

During the early morning hours of August 31, the joint BOP-FBI tactical team stormed the prison building occupied by the inmates. All nine hostages were safely rescued, and no prisoners were injured despite the use of breaching explosives. The mission was as difficult as any Bill had ever experienced. Without a doubt, the cooperation and collaboration of the BOP and FBI personnel were the real reasons for its success.

The exigency of the circumstances at Talladega illustrates how important it is for leaders to be able to define a common mission, put aside self-interests, and work together, quickly and effectively. When harmony between agencies does not exist or cannot be developed, a volatile situation can worsen. In their capacity as the incident commanders, had the wardens and FBI executives not immediately recognized the need for total cooperation, a second, and possibly worse, crisis would have occurred—a crisis of leadership.

- Every individual, group, or organization has its strengths and weaknesses, but as you work together, the merging of those strengths easily overcomes the individual weaknesses.
- Pride and solidarity are essential elements of a highly motivated workforce, but a leader must be careful to see that conceit and insularity do not inhibit the cooperative spirit necessary to thrive as an organization.
- A wise leader will balance institutional honor with humility to develop essential partnerships.

THIRTEEN

Help! I Need Somebody

Agent Anthony "Andy" M. Gonzalez was barely out of the FBI's Training Academy in Quantico when, on a hot, muggy afternoon in a North Miami Beach parking lot, he found himself facing a stranger aiming a handgun directly at him.

Moments earlier, Andy had returned from a quick lunch with fellow agents and parked his car in the fenced, open-air lot adjacent to the FBI's Miami area headquarters. As he stepped out of the FBI car, Andy noticed a man he did not recognize running across the parking lot. The runner was carrying a bag that looked similar to the gym bags many FBI agents kept in their cars, some full of workout gear, others containing extra clothing or crime scene investigation tools.

Things weren't adding up in those quick moments. Andy didn't recognize the man as a fellow FBI employee, and he was moving quickly as if to avoid confrontation. It was quite likely he had just stolen the bag out of one of the employees' cars. Andy yelled at the man, commanding him to halt. The man paid no heed and continued to sprint across the parking lot until he reached the fence that enclosed it on the west. On the other side of the fence was a different parking lot, this one belonging to an apartment building. The man managed to scramble up the fence and jump down to the other side without dropping the bag.

Adrenaline kicking in, Andy rapidly scaled the fence after the stranger, followed seconds later by FBI agent Paul Jacobson, who happened to arrive at the FBI parking lot shortly after Andy did. As Andy reached the apartment building's parking lot, he called out again, identifying himself as a law enforcement officer and directing the runner to stop. This time the man did stop and deliberately turned toward Andy. As he pivoted, he reached into the bag he still carried, swiftly withdrew a handgun, aimed it at Andy, and fired.

Andy reacted as he had been taught and quickly drew his own weapon. Untouched by the assailant's bullet, Andy was able to fire his own gun at the attacker to protect himself and Agent Jacobson. Hit by Andy's bullet, the unidentified man went down immediately and now lay fatally wounded. His bag, filled with a number of disguises and additional ammunition for his pistol, had also fallen to the ground. Later Andy would learn that his potential killer was a suspect in a number of bank robberies. Ironically, his photograph was on Andy's desk back at the FBI office.

No shooting by a law enforcement officer is considered routine, and the required administrative reviews that follow—though necessary—can be intimidating and worrisome. FBI procedures require that anyone who fires a gun in the line of duty must immediately surrender it, creating the immediate perception by some that the agent's actions must have been wrong. Walking away from the scene of a shooting without a weapon can cause those involved to believe they have lost the confidence of their superiors. For others, the situation is tantamount to becoming powerless.

Once an "agent-involved" shooting has been reviewed by internal investigators (a process that can take months) and the actions are found to be justified, the agent's gun is returned. The real reason for surrendering the weapon is, of course, to conduct the necessary ballistics examinations, preserve evidence, and protect those involved in the shooting. At the time, the FBI policies pertaining to agent-involved shootings were improving, and internal investigators were being instructed on the potential psychological impact of the fact-finding process on employees and their families.

News about shootings, injuries, and deaths travels at lightning speed in the FBI. On the day of this shooting, Kathleen McChesney was managing the Executive Development and Selection Program at FBI Headquarters when she learned that an agent-involved shooting had occurred in Miami. Kathleen and her work partners were relieved that no FBI employees had been harmed.

Late that afternoon, Kathleen joined a group of men and women who were having coffee in the FBI's half-empty cafeteria discussing the incident in

Miami. One of the most professionally and emotionally fulfilling experiences in the FBI is the vicarious satisfaction and pride one feels in a job well done. They commended the success of their fellow agent. One senior executive at the crowded table was particularly animated in describing the actions of the SAC of the Miami office, Bill Gavin. Next to the actions of the agents involved in a critical situation, it is the performance of the SAC that comes under the most scrutiny.

"Gavin gave the kid his own gun!" exclaimed the executive, referring to Andy Gonzalez, his voice filled with admiration as well as astonishment. Kathleen pictured Bill Gavin, whom she knew slightly, arriving at the scene of the shooting and doing what FBI commanders do—taking charge of the situation, exerting control, and looking out for the employees and citizens involved. Everyone at the table was familiar with similar agent-involved shooting situations where weapons were taken from the agents who fired them, but none had ever heard of an SAC actually giving his own gun to the agent involved in the shooting.

In retrospect, Bill Gavin's action may seem minor, but in the organizational subculture of the FBI at that time, his demonstration of concern was perhaps unique, and the story was retold often as an example of consideration and compassion. It is apparent to even the most disagreeable armchair quarterbacks that an executive who understands the feelings of his or her subordinates, particularly in a traumatic situation, is an exceptional leader.

In the FBI's lengthy history, many men and women have demonstrated the ability to take charge of a difficult situation and still remain attuned to the emotional needs of their employees. Often new leaders mistakenly believe that being responsible and being compassionate are mutually exclusive characteristics. To the contrary, these are two of the most indispensable and interrelated attributes of a good leader.

- Recognize when employees need personal assistance and know how to provide it without undue interference.
- Help your employees maintain their self-respect and protect their privacy when they encounter difficult circumstances.
- Offer aid to peers who appear to be struggling.

FOURTEEN

It Is Your Business

There are a lot of FBI agents like "Kyle"—a great investigator and self-starter—the type of agent that every supervisor treasures. He mentored new agents on his squad and taught them the importance of paying attention to every detail of their cases. His coworkers admired his irreproachable work ethic, but it was his engaging smile that immediately endeared him to you. Happily married to his college sweetheart and the father of two teenage children, he was often heard to exclaim, "Life is good!" to everyone, or to no one in particular.

As sometimes happens to good people, Kyle's personality and behavior began to change in little ways, and the quality of his work slowly deteriorated. Where he was once reliable, his behavior was now unpredictable. He began to take more sick days than usual, although he did not appear to have a serious illness. When he did come to work, he would arrive early in the morning, stay for a few minutes, and then leave. He rarely returned to the office in the afternoon, which was contrary to the common practice of the other agents. This affable and engaging man had become quiet, removed, and disconnected from his fellow squad members.

One day Kyle's supervisor told his SAC that he believed that Kyle was ready for a change of assignment and asked that Kyle be transferred to a different squad. Sometimes supervisors use this reasoning to transfer a nonperforming agent to another squad, but from what the SAC knew of Kyle's work it seemed unlikely that he was a slacker. The SAC wanted to find out more about Kyle's situation before he made a decision. He pressed the supervisor and others about Kyle's recent behavior.

Much to his chagrin, the SAC learned from the supervisor and by interviewing others who knew Kyle that he had been out sick for several days and that some of his squad mates were covering for him while he was attempting to resolve whatever issues he had. To make matters worse, Kyle was leaving home every morning at his usual time, leading his wife to believe that he was going to work. Instead of coming to the office, however, he would drive to an unobtrusive spot, park his car, and drink beer. After a while he found a bar that was open in the mornings and started hanging out there during the workday.

At the time, the FBI did not have a program to assist agents with alcoholism or substance abuse problems. Nonetheless, the SAC knew that in order to save Kyle, he needed to initiate an intervention on his behalf. This process involved Kyle's wife and oldest child, his parish priest, a counselor, a representative from a rehabilitative facility, one of his closest friends, and, in this case, the SAC. Though Kyle was shocked and embarrassed to be confronted in this way, he agreed to immediately enter an alcohol rehabilitation program. He knew that without help, he would be unable to take control over his life, rebuild his self-esteem, and regain the confidence of his family and friends.

Although Kyle's problems were a private matter, news of his extended absence traveled quickly through the office. Agents looking for the facts soon found out that the SAC had been responsible for, and involved in, the intervention. Many of Kyle's squad mates felt that the head of their office should not have interfered in Kyle's personal life. They had seen fellow agents with similar problems before, and those issues appeared to have been resolved without official interference. Embracing this particular point of view was the group's first collective mistake.

Their second mistake was to send three representatives from the squad to confront the SAC. These agents felt it was important to let their boss know that this intervention was unnecessary and that he should have stayed out of their friend's private affairs. The SAC met with the trio, but he would not discuss any details of the intervention with them. Instead, he took the opportunity to point out that since each of them had apparently been aware that their fellow agent was in distress, they had seriously failed him by their inaction. Furthermore, the SAC suggested that they owed Kyle and his family an apology for not caring enough to assist him in overcoming his addiction.

Two months later Kyle returned to work, healthier and much like his old self. Shortly after his return, the SAC passed through his work area at the end of a workday as the squad members were returning from their investigations. Kyle stood up from his chair and walked up to the SAC. No one knew what to expect—perhaps Kyle was angry with him or wanted to show his peers that he could deal with him publicly. The entire squad, including those agents who had criticized the SAC, watched with surprise as Kyle put his arms around him and hugged him.

"Thanks for all that you did, Boss," Kyle said. "You saved me, and you saved my family."

Not long after Kyle's intervention, the FBI implemented an employee assistance program that has helped troubled employees deal with significant personal afflictions. Without this assistance, their problems could have led to unprofessional behavior and perhaps to the loss of their jobs. Fortunately, many companies have now established their own similar programs or contracted with private health care groups to provide these critical services.

Although the FBI's formal employee assistance program wasn't available for Kyle, this resourceful SAC was able to find professional services to help him. Over time, Kyle's peers came to the conclusion that the SAC's involvement in Kyle's situation had been an act of leadership and compassion. Despite the awkwardness of the situation, helping this employee regain his health and self-esteem was the right thing to do and unquestionably well worth the effort.

- It is your business as a leader to recognize when a coworker, a superior, or a subordinate needs help in dealing with a demon that is impacting his or her work or health.
- With due regard to their privacy and dignity, you should connect troubled colleagues with professional employee assistance.
- Regardless of the kindness a leader may bestow or how valuable the result, there may always be someone who believes the leader has overstepped the boundary between superior and subordinate.

FIFTEEN

The Boss Is Not Always Right

New supervisors face dozens of leadership challenges every day. "Terry" received a coveted assignment in a midwestern FBI office as the first-line supervisor of a squad of twelve agents. The varied investigative responsibilities of the squad—including kidnapping, extortion, bank robbery, theft from interstate shipments, and interstate transportation of stolen property—made her role even more challenging and exciting. The agents were well-seasoned investigators who produced excellent results in solving the cases assigned to them.

As the new supervisor, Terry felt it was important to get to know all of the agents and identify their strengths and weaknesses and likes and dislikes, so that she could make appropriate work assignments. As she did that, she determined which squad members the others turned to for assistance with their cases. There are usually one or two of these "alpha" agents on every squad who function as an unofficial supervisor, and they can be particularly helpful to a new supervisor. Terry also talked with her fellow managers about the reputation of the individuals on the squad and the quality of their work.

Supervisors can learn a great deal about their subordinates if they take the time to listen and observe the nonverbal communication among them. Watching the squad members interact with agents from other squads gave Terry the additional information that she needed to be an effective and productive manager. Socializing appropriately with them provided the final dynamic in the process of becoming their leader.

"Mitch," one of the agents assigned to the squad, was a management challenge from the day Terry arrived. Large and mildly aggressive by nature, he never missed an occasion to explain that he usually did whatever he wanted because the bosses were intimidated by him. This was not the best way to start out with Terry, but she gave him a little room, hoping that he would recognize the importance of being a team player and work with her. He was a distraction but also quite capable.

Mitch's behavior often bordered on insubordination, but he would usually pull back just short of it. On one occasion he crossed that line in front of the other members of the squad, and Terry knew it was time to break his habit of churlish behavior. She called his bluff by giving him a direct order to keep his rude comments to himself. To the surprise of some, he didn't know what to do—other than to do as Terry directed or suffer the consequences. Although Terry hadn't done or said anything to demean him, Mitch was embarrassed in front of his peers, who clearly felt the tension. Needless to say, Terry and Mitch did not become fast friends, but he continued to do all that was required of him.

Some months later, the squad was about to enter an important phase of an undercover operation, and Terry called the group together for a meeting in her office. She explained to them how she wanted this particular part of the project handled and went over her plan in minute detail. When she finished presenting her ideas, she asked the agents if they agreed with her. They all nodded their assent—except for Mitch, who just sat there, scowling.

Terry asked Mitch if he had some other thoughts about her strategy. She pointed out that if he did, he should put them on the table. Mitch simply said, "You're the boss. We'll do it your way."

Terry decided to prod Mitch to tell his coworkers if he had a plan that would work better than the one that she had just offered. She politely pointed out that if Mitch's ideas were superior to hers, his fellow squad members deserved to hear them.

Mitch reluctantly agreed to share his plan with the group. As he laid out each element of his proposal, it was obvious that he had hit a home run. Terry's plan never would have had the chance of producing the results that Mitch's plan would. She immediately suggested that the squad follow Mitch's plan instead of hers—a recommendation that surprised Mitch and was readily accepted by the other squad members.

While Terry and Mitch never became close associates, their mutual respect grew and their working relationship improved. Some years later Mitch told Terry that he really didn't think she would let him win that day. Terry told him that they both won that day because his plan was the best way to reach their goal.

A leader hopes that by the time his or her management skills and leadership abilities have been recognized and a management position achieved, he or she will make only the best possible decisions. One capable enough to lead, however, also should be realistic and mature enough to know it is impossible to always be right. The incident with Mitch confirmed for Terry that her ideas weren't always the best ones. Had she not urged him to speak up and run the risk of being overshadowed, the team would have lost its best opportunity to be successful. As important, she garnered a great deal of admiration from her subordinates by encouraging them to speak their minds and by adopting Mitch's idea because it was superior to hers.

TO LISTEN AND RESPECT

Unlike Terry, two other FBI leaders lost the respect of their subordinates by failing to consider their suggestions or treat them with dignity. "Super-Agent-in-Charge," as he liked to call himself, thought he knew everything there was to know about FBI work. Early in Kathleen's FBI career, while auditing an undercover operation that he supervised, she politely pointed out how he was not following established policy for a particular accounting procedure. Instead of asking to see the policy, he berated her for accusing him of being wrong. Even after she showed him the rule, he asserted that he did not intend to follow a rule he had not seen.

Some years later Kathleen found herself working for Super-Agent-in-Charge. During a critical strategy session in the investigation of a kidnapping of a baby, she recommended to him that a specially equipped airplane with infrared imaging capabilities was needed to follow possible suspects and look for the child. Super-Agent-in-Charge rudely dismissed her suggestion in front of her subordinates and peers, claiming the equipment wasn't necessary. His cold demeanor was an embarrassment to everyone in the room.

A few hours later, Super-Agent-in-Charge announced that he had come up with an idea to use an airplane in the case. Though he had come around to Kathleen's way of thinking, his poor leadership skills in a life-threatening situation firmly convinced her that the boss is not always right or professional and that everyone's ideas should be respectfully heard.

Another manager, the "Muffin Man," was oblivious to many things, including the fact that he appeared extremely condescending toward women in the workplace. Perhaps thinking that women appreciated his attention, he gave his female coworkers demeaning nicknames such as "Peach Muffin" and "Raisin Muffin" and frequently called them by those names in public. Consequently, these women, and most of their male coworkers, developed an undeserved low opinion of Muffin Man and even created a demeaning nickname for him that they used outside of his presence.

When Kathleen discovered Muffin Man's idiosyncrasy and the negative impact it had on employee morale and productivity, she spoke with him about it. She explained how his words were being perceived and was able to convince him to start addressing his employees professionally and to drop the juvenile nicknames. In his defense, Muffin Man said he did not intend to degrade these women because he truly believed that they enjoyed the personal attention he provided. Nevertheless, as their leader he should have recognized and dealt with their growing impatience with him.

- Look for and draw out the talent in your team.
- Be humble enough to acknowledge when you are wrong and your subordinates are right.
- The real win is a successful result.

SIXTEEN

No Good Deed Goes Unpunished

The old, well-known movie line "Don't shoot, G-Men!" established "G-Man" as the pop culture nickname for an FBI agent. This distinctive description has endured since the 1930s when FBI agents were first authorized to carry guns. Over the years that followed, the FBI developed world-class firearms training courses for all types of weapons, ranging from nonlethal devices to high-powered automatic rifles. Through its firearms program, the FBI also evaluates ammunition, protective equipment, and training methods, and it shares its findings with the law enforcement community.

FBI agents are required to establish their firearms proficiency several times each year. During these sessions, agents also learn new skills in order to keep up with changes in firearm equipment and technology. More important, they review the laws and recent court cases regarding the use of firearms to become as knowledgeable about when to shoot as how to shoot.

"Mike" was a former Marine captain with distinguished service in the first Gulf War, one of many veterans who have joined the FBI. The Bureau suited Mike's outgoing personality, and he enjoyed the immediate camaraderie of working with a squad of investigators. He also found the FBI structure an easy environment in which to work and was impressed with the emphasis that the FBI placed on continuous training for its employees.

Mike was assigned to work on a squad that investigated bank robberies and extortions and arrested fugitives. He enjoyed locating and apprehending the bad guys, but he also loved teaching. The other firearms instructors readily accepted Mike's offer to help out on the range, where he quickly gained high regard for his knowledge of firearms and his low-key teaching style. He earned special praise from a group of seasoned, but reluctant, agents whom he taught to use the semiautomatic pistols that would replace their familiar revolvers.

A few FBI field offices have their own firearms range, but most offices conduct training at a shared facility. In Mike's field office, the lead firearms instructor had negotiated a long-term agreement with a branch of the military to use one of its ranges in return for maintaining the range. A few months after the agreement was signed, this lead instructor retired, and Kathleen asked Mike to consider taking over these important responsibilities.

Mike was concerned that his peers might find his FBI experience to be too limited for him to take on this role, but when several senior agents on his squad encouraged him, he enthusiastically accepted the offer. His transition to this leadership position proved to be an easy one, as he was organized and innovative and his counterparts appreciated his down-to-earth nature. As his superior, Kathleen McChesney had heard good things about Mike's work and his lack of FBI seniority seemed to be easily overcome by his military experience and maturity.

One Friday afternoon during his first year in his new role, Mike came to see Kathleen. When he arrived at the office, she could immediately tell that something was wrong. This happy-go-lucky man looked lost, sad, and alone.

"I think I may have screwed up, and I don't know what to do," he said slowly.

Unless they have no conscience, most people feel bad when they have made a mistake, particularly one that may impact others. Breaking a rule or doing something perceived as wrong is often painful for FBI agents, because they are not expected to err. Mike was too upset to sit down, so Kathleen stood up.

"It can't be that bad," she said. Thinking of the worst-case scenario she added, "You didn't kill anybody, did you?"

Mike didn't laugh or smile. "No, it's none of that. But I may be in big trouble. I may have caused trouble for the other instructors and for you, too."

"Well, let's talk about what you think you did wrong, and then we can figure out how to fix it."

"OK," Mike began. "You know how when we finish shooting at the range and we pick up the ejected ammo brass?"

Thousands of these cartridge casings fall to the ground every time there is a firearms qualification or training day. Typically, the agents pick them up and throw them into plastic barrels. Later, the firearms instructors remove the brass from the range, a task that few agents know or think about.

"For months I've been selling the used brass and using the money to buy supplies for the SWAT team," Mike continued. "I just heard from an instructor at the FBI Academy that I am not supposed to do that. Apparently someone at the Academy is pretty upset that I didn't send the money to them or to FBI Headquarters."

Kathleen could see that Mike was anguished by the possibility that he had done something that could tarnish his good name or cause his peers to lose faith in his ability to lead. "What's the brass worth?" she asked.

"I know exactly how much it was—around $200. I kept records of all of this. I'll pay it if I screwed up. I didn't mean to do anything wrong," Mike replied.

"Let me check this out," she said. "Give me some time to think about who to talk with."

The next day Kathleen called Mike at home to see how he was doing and to tell him that she would contact an FBI official who would know how to deal with the situation. On Monday she reached a colleague in the Office of Professional Responsibility (OPR), the FBI's internal investigative component. She told him what Mike had done and asked for some guidance.

"He shouldn't have done that" was the official's first response.

"I can understand why he shouldn't have done this," Kathleen replied, "but he didn't know that he shouldn't. There is no specific rule about processing used brass. Furthermore, what he did was to help, in a very small way, our SWAT team program. It makes perfect sense to me."

In hopes of avoiding a protracted and unnecessary internal investigation, Kathleen set up a conference call with a finance officer, an ethics officer, and her colleague from the OPR. During the call she explained that Mike had immediately come forward about the matter and had procedures put in place to remit the proceeds from the spent brass to FBI Headquarters in the future.

She also pointed out that Mike did not personally benefit from what he had done.

One of the harder heads on the call spoke up. "Well, as a firearms instructor, he's supposed to know what to do regardless of the existence of a written rule."

"He's a new firearms instructor and just didn't think about this. That does not mean he intended to do something wrong," Kathleen argued.

"But are you sure he's got records for the sale of the brass?" someone else asked.

"Yes, I am. I have had an accountant look at them," she answered, hoping not to sound as irritated as she was. "Mike brought this matter to the attention of this office, and I'm bringing it to your attention. We're correcting it, and I'm asking you not to punish Mike for an honest mistake." Finally reason prevailed, and everyone on the call agreed that this situation called for clarification and training rather than severe discipline.

Later that day, Mike came in to see Kathleen and find out what she had heard from FBI Headquarters. He had the same sad look on his face as before and the sweat on his forehead was visible. He leaned against the doorway as if he might need it for support. "Am I going to lose my job?" he wanted to know.

"Not at all," Kathleen said. "You were trying to do something good for your fellow agents and broke a rule you didn't know about. You had a logical and efficient idea, but there was an established system for handling the brass. No good deed—"

"Goes unpunished," Mike finished her thought.

He finally sat down, clearly relieved.

"Thank you," he mumbled. "I . . . well . . . I just thank you."

- Any good intention can backfire.
- Leaders perform good deeds, regardless of the possibility of unexpected negative consequences.
- Maintain an internal disciplinary process in your organization that is just and reasonable.

SEVENTEEN

Defend Your Team

"It turned to shit! We shot the guy!" Henry said.

Those were not the words Sheri Farrar expected to hear. Her second in command, Henry Ragle, was in Columbus, Ohio, with the Cincinnati field office's SWAT team directing a drug sting. Although Sheri had been the office's SAC for less than a month, she knew Henry very well and had confidence in him to conduct the operation without her direct oversight or involvement. Henry was in a hotel room when he called to tell her what had happened.

At first Sheri thought Henry was kidding. "Very funny, Henry," she replied.

"No, no—I mean it!" Henry said. "He's shot through the arm. Our team is okay, though."

Sheri had been watching the clock all afternoon and hoping to hear about the successful arrest of a narcotics dealer. Before Henry finally reached her, she was becoming concerned that the operation was taking too long, but she was still surprised at the turn of events. She told Henry to bring the team over to the Columbus office, where she would meet up with them.

It took Sheri less than the normal two hours to get from Cincinnati to Columbus. On the way she called FBI Headquarters to report the shooting and initiate the mandatory internal investigation of the incident. Sheri was authorized to assemble available leaders from nearby offices to conduct this inquiry. By the time she arrived in Columbus, she had located supervisors in Cleveland and Louisville who were available to assist.

Though she had met many of the Cincinnati agents already, Sheri had not worked with any of them. She assumed, correctly, that they would be judging her words and actions to see if she measured up to their idea of a leader. When she got to the Columbus office, she immediately approached the agent who had fired the shot that hit the suspect. She asked him how he was doing and then asked the same of the other members of the group. After she gathered some key facts about what had occurred, she carefully explained the internal inquiry process that follows a shooting incident and the reasons for it. Knowing that the team was anxious about being second-guessed by others, she tried to put their minds at ease by focusing on a positive outcome.

Sheri sent the team home for the evening and then accompanied Henry to the drug dealer's house, where other agents were executing a search warrant. As expected, illegal narcotics and a substantial amount of money were found. It was a long night, but the evidence they discovered was crucial to the suspect's subsequent guilty plea to drug possession.

When the inquiry team arrived the following day, Sheri learned that an official at FBI Headquarters had instructed the investigators not to provide any administrative warnings to the SWAT team members they were about to interview. This meant that the agents involved in the shooting would not be told that they were compelled to provide statements as a matter of their employment. Use of the administrative warnings ensures that any compelled statement cannot be used in a personnel action against the employee, or in any criminal proceeding, which is important in the event that someone later suspects criminal culpability on the part of a SWAT team member.

Sheri immediately stopped the inquiry and contacted the official at headquarters who had given those instructions. She reminded him that this was not a criminal action and told him that if he insisted that the agents not receive administrative warnings, she would inform them that they were not compelled to give any statements whatsoever. She went on to tell the official that if anyone tried to use any statement that the agents might give without being properly advised of the nature of the inquiry, she would be the first to testify to the impropriety. When she finished, the official realized that Sheri was correct in her assessment and in looking out for her employees at a very critical time. He agreed that the inquiry team would provide the appropriate administrative warnings to the agents before the interviews.

Before Sheri's arrival in Columbus following the shooting, a few of the members of the SWAT team had been concerned about what Sheri might say or do. They were not yet familiar with her as their leader and were worried that because she had no experience with them she might not back their actions. Some even thought that she might be angry with them for the way things went down. Their concerns were dispelled, however, not only by her concern for their well-being but especially by the actions that she took to make certain that the internal inquiry into their shooting incident was conducted fairly and professionally.

- Select and develop subordinates in whom you have confidence, as it is nearly impossible for a leader to be a part of every critical operation.
- Protect your employees from any misguided or improper inquiry about their work or actions.
- Be a calming, confident influence on employees who must defend their work or actions to others.
- Stand up for your employees when they have acted properly, but do not neglect them if they err.

EIGHTEEN

Your Own Worst Enemy

Rigorous background checks and stringent hiring standards generally help to ensure that only the most ethical and mature men and women are chosen to become FBI agents. However, despite the careful and thorough selection process, a small number of agents have been hired whose character flaws or personal problems caused them to act in ways so egregious that they were fired from the FBI.

Some of these agents were highly admired men and women within the Bureau before they fell into financial difficulties and mistakenly believed that their only way out was to accept money from criminals. Others were narcissistic, selfish people who lacked any conscience or moral grounding. Others got caught in the downward spiral of alcoholism and a very small number even committed crimes ranging from minor theft to espionage and even murder. Regardless of the reasons, these agents became their own worst enemies through their own actions and made it necessary for the FBI to investigate its own employees.

Agents Steven Travis and Alan Rotton were likable, popular men who lived somewhat on the edge of the FBI family. Although they were involved in all of the cases and social activities of the Kansas City FBI office, they seemed to believe that they were smarter and better than their peers—that is, until their lives came crashing down. In the end, it was difficult for their peers to believe that these two men would betray all of their friends, their coworkers, and their country. By their poor decisions and subsequent actions they destroyed their own lives and those of their families and sadly tarnished the FBI badge.

As all FBI agents do, Travis and Rotton took an oath to uphold and defend the Constitution and the laws of the United States. As part of that responsibility, they investigated federal crimes and brought the offenders to court to be held accountable for their offenses. They became partners, cultivated informants to strengthen their cases, and worked well with other law enforcement agencies and corporate security managers. Over time, they developed hundreds of cases involving cargo theft and different types of stolen property in western Missouri and eastern Kansas. They were looked up to by other agents for their investigative successes and their ability to gather useful, crime-solving information from many of the criminals they had arrested. Travis and Rotton also befriended some of the managers in the field office, which, unfortunately, led to an overestimation of Rotton's leadership ability. Management influence and his own ambition gained Rotton a promotion and transfer to FBI Headquarters.

For most of their years of working together, Travis had played second fiddle to Rotton's stronger personality and had succumbed to his manipulative nature. Rotton's abrupt move left Travis without a mentor. Without Rotton's cover and protection, it did not take long for their web of criminal activity to begin to unravel.

The trouble for Travis and Rotton began when a longtime, trusted FBI informant warned his agent-handler that the Kansas City office had a serious internal problem. While hesitant at first to provide details, the informant finally revealed that Travis and Rotton were using one of their own informants to help them deal in stolen goods.

This serious allegation against two FBI agents was not easy for the agent-handler or his supervisor to believe. Bill Gavin, who had only recently been assigned as the office's assistant special agent in charge, realized it was critical that this information be swiftly verified or proven false. He authorized a review of the office telephone records and from them discovered that Rotton, now working hundreds of miles away in Washington, D.C., was in constant communication with Travis. Furthermore, as a few handpicked agents analyzed current theft reports, it looked as if Travis and Rotton might still be involved in criminal activity.

It was difficult to conduct a surveillance of Travis because he knew all of the agents in the office. To deal with that problem, SAC Lee Laster brought in agents from other FBI offices, whom Travis did not know, to follow him around the clock. It didn't take long before these skilled surveillance agents saw Travis involved in suspicious activity that reinforced the information provided by the informant. These observations and Travis's continued contact with Rotton led to the next investigative step—to seek a federal court order for a wiretap on both of their telephones.

Intrusive wiretap surveillance is not employed without great consideration. When successful, this technique provides excellent proof of criminal activity and intent. Before the actual request for a wiretap is made to a judge, investigators have to document facts that create a basis for the probable cause that a crime is being planned or is currently under way. They also have to affirm that all other logical investigative methods have been tried and were unsuccessful in reaching the objective of gathering absolute proof of criminal activity.

This particular wiretap would be the first ever used against FBI agents in their homes or offices. Top-level lawyers in the U.S. attorneys' offices in Missouri, Kansas, Virginia, and Washington, D.C., as well as FBI director William H. Webster and U.S. Attorney General William French Smith, carefully reviewed the documents supporting the unprecedented request. Everyone knew that if the allegations were proven to be true, the image of the FBI would be harmed. Regardless of the black eye that might result from the investigation, the more important aspect of the case was to demonstrate to the public and other FBI employees that the Bureau aggressively and responsibly deals with internal acts of impropriety or criminality.

As with Travis's surveillance, the sensitivity of his ongoing employment in the Kansas City office made it impossible for his coworkers to listen to and record his or Rotton's conversations. Once the court approved the installation of the wiretaps, the SAC again borrowed agents from other FBI offices to work covertly in Kansas City and gather information from the conversations.

After a few days of secretly listening to their conversations, it was clear to the agents that Travis and Rotton were still involved in criminal activity and what their modus operandi was. First, Rotton would contact a railroad investigator friend with whom he had worked in the past. This investigator trusted Rotton and would innocently talk with him about new railroad procedures in place to prevent theft or casually tell him the locations of railroad cars containing high-value merchandise. Rotton would then relay this information to Travis in Kansas City. Travis, in turn, contacted their accomplice who would set up the merchandise to be stolen by other thieves. Finally, Travis and Rotton made arrangements with the accomplice to share the proceeds from the sale of the stolen goods.

FBI director Webster took a personal interest in this investigation and had frequent conversations with those managing this sensitive case. Nonetheless, everyone was surprised when the director came to Kansas City for other business and asked to meet with the agents who were listening to and analyzing Travis and Rotton's phone calls.

As a former federal judge, Director Webster was very knowledgeable about the legal process associated with wiretaps, but he had not witnessed the actual monitoring of telephone conversations. In this case, the agents were working in a substandard warehouse in a high-crime neighborhood that was chosen for its accessibility to telephone equipment. The location and building structure presented some challenges for the visit of a public figure, but on the day of his visit the director was discreetly driven into the warehouse, where he walked through its filthy basement and up a set of broken stairs to see the listening post.

The agents were as eager to meet the director as he was to see them. As he shook hands with everyone, he thanked them for their dedication and the time they were spending away from their friends and families to work on this case. More important, he spoke to the issues at hand, reminding the agents that without the integrity of its people and its commitment to investigate its own people when necessary, the FBI could not maintain the public's trust and confidence.

Despite everyone's diligence in keeping the knowledge of the case limited to those who needed to know, Travis and Rotton began to suspect that an investigation was under way. To impede the investigation, they planned a retaliatory action against one of the investigators. Although their plans were discovered and neutralized, it was obvious that these formerly good men would stop at nothing to extricate themselves from the situation that they had created.

The information from the recordings of the Travis-Rotton conversations was used to obtain arrest warrants for them and search warrants for their homes. On the day of the searches, an agent contacted Mrs. Travis and suggested that she take her young children out of the house to spare them the ordeal of watching strangers go through their rooms. Among the many items of stolen property retrieved from their residence, it was a bicycle that Travis had foolishly given to his son that most clearly illustrated the impact of what he had done.

When the case ended, SAC Laster explained the reasons for the confidentiality to the employees who had not been privy to the information earlier. Although some felt slighted that they had not been considered trustworthy, most of them appreciated Laster's ultimate candor. They came to realize that one innocent slip could have compromised the investigation and that the secrecy had been necessary to prevent that from happening. The SAC also gave everyone in the office copies of the documents used to initiate and perpetuate the investigation. This was particularly important for the fence-sitters who needed to see the evidence against their former friends for themselves before they could believe that such a thing was true.

The day that Travis and Rotton were arrested was a very sad one for the FBI family. Colleagues questioned why two family men with prestigious jobs would risk everything for a small amount of money. Steve Travis pleaded guilty and was sent to federal prison, where he lived among some of the men he had had a part in incarcerating. More tragically, Al Rotton took his own life before their trial.

Though painfully embarrassing, the Travis-Rotton case reinforced the importance of maintaining high standards of conduct for all FBI employees. The actions of the FBI leaders demonstrated that they would pursue internal problems as they would any other federal crime—with honesty and vigor.

- Maintaining the integrity of any organization is a special responsibility of its leaders.
- Strong core values and enforceable standards of conduct are absolutely essential in sustaining an organization, though their existence does not guarantee that people will not find ways to derail their own careers.
- Unethical behavior in an organization must be addressed aggressively through timely and thorough investigation, and findings of wrongdoing must be followed by appropriate consequences.

NINETEEN

Respect the Boss—Regardless

Employees frequently develop terms or sayings that characterize an organizational process or procedure in a unique way. These special clichés provide workers with a way to rationalize their actions and remarks, to reinforce their identification with the group, and to strengthen internal bonds.

An often used FBI term that describes someone who is eligible to retire is "KMA," based on a well-known vulgarism. The individual who is in KMA status is thought to be unconcerned about speaking or acting out because, if criticized, he or she can quickly and easily leave the organization with the pension intact. The employee, particularly a leader, who thinks that KMA status affords him or her the right to publicly express opinions about superiors without possible career ramifications should pay close attention to "Alex's" story.

Even before reaching his KMA status, Alex had no trouble voicing his opinions. As he worked his way up the FBI's promotion ladder to field office SAC, he occasionally shocked the other agents with his brusque appraisals of a situation or foe. Alex was smart enough, however, to keep his well-founded criticisms to himself or at least to keep them "in house."

Positive relationships with members of the media are good for the FBI, and Alex had a friendly, confident relationship with the local press. Journalists could count on him for a great sound bite or piece of information that would help them develop or enhance a story. It was no surprise, then, that when Alex's boss became involved in an intriguing public controversy, several reporters were eager to question him about it.

Alex had strong feelings about the way his boss had handled the issue in question, and, as it turned out, his evaluations were correct. When he shared his thoughts about his boss with a reporter during the course of an interview on another subject, his remarks made their way into the next day's newspapers. When Alex's boss and other FBI Headquarters officials read the story and confirmed that he had openly criticized his leader, they took swift action and temporarily suspended him from his position. Alex stood by his remarks because they were true, but his superiors now perceived him to be unprofessional and disrespectful.

TOO MUCH CANDOR

Another coworker "Jay" had an equally candid moment with his boss, and like Alex, his perceptions of the issues were precise and true. Jay was assigned to a special task force investigating one of the FBI's most complex, long-term cases because he was considered one of the "best of the best" among FBI agents. His technical skills and willingness to work long hours made him a very important part of the team, and he loved the challenges the work presented.

The most important FBI cases have enormous administrative burdens, especially the preparation and delivery of briefings and status updates to senior leaders. Although these presentations are the best way to obtain additional personnel and other resources for the case and to demonstrate the talents of the team members, they are time consuming. They also require some diplomacy.

During one of these special case assignments, Jay and his fellow task force members spent several days helping their supervisor prepare a briefing that he would present to the prosecutors assigned to the case. The team carefully outlined their boss's presentation, and Jay even helped him practice his verbal delivery so that it would be flawless.

When the time came to deliver his remarks, Jay's boss was confident and in command of the facts. He articulately recited detail after detail as if putting building blocks together and made a convincing structure of guilt. The lawyers seemed impressed with the evidence that the task force had gathered.

After the presentation, the agents met back in their office to share their observations. Jay's boss was clearly happy with his performance, and several investigators congratulated him with handshakes and pats on the back. Obviously he had done well and was enjoying the moment and, perhaps, the praise as well.

As the session ended and the team members began to leave the office, the boss asked Jay for his opinion on his presentation. Jay, who had been silent until then, assumed that his boss really wanted to know his thoughts, so he pulled a card out of his pocket on which he had scribbled some notes about the briefing.

"I think you could have been more forceful," he began, and to illustrate his impression he recited a list of points that he believed his boss had neglected or failed to make soundly.

Jay's boss was shocked, as were the other agents in the room who overheard the conversation. The boss had just been lauded by the other investigators, and now Jay was throwing cold water on the moment. To Jay, this was all about the business at hand, but, for his boss, it was a communication gone awry.

In his uncomplimentary litany, Jay offered some sound opinions that neither his boss nor the other team members had mentioned. Unfortunately, in speaking so candidly to his boss in front of his subordinates, Jay had chosen the wrong time and place to deliver his message. He had also communicated from a negative point of view, disregarding any positive aspects of the presentation and focusing directly on the missteps. So deeply focused on the case, Jay failed to recognize the personal dynamics of the characters in this drama until it was too late.

To no one's surprise, the relationship between Jay and his boss was never the same after that incident. Although they continued to work together effectively, Jay's boss and those who overheard the comments did not forget his surprising comments. To make matters worse, one of the agents was so astonished by Jay's actions that he shared this story with others and caused some harm to Jay's otherwise unblemished professional reputation. Years later, when Jay was seeking a promotion, one of the agents who was present at the critique declined to endorse him, describing this particular event as indicative of Jay's "lack of interpersonal skills and judgment."

Notwithstanding the accuracy of one's conclusions, sharing your personal opinions about your leader's actions is risky, even if your boss asks for your candid opinion—and especially if you make an off-the-record remark to a "trusted" newsman. Although the most articulate leader can misspeak or be misinterpreted, in Alex's case he wasn't misquoted and his meaning was clear. Though the truth is often thought of as one's best defense, Alex's discipline and Jay's promotion difficulties were strong reminders about avoiding the impulse to publicly criticize one's boss or coworkers.

- Avoid the temptation to criticize others in public—even if you are right.
- Criticism is best received when delivered privately, respectfully, and constructively.
- Leaders know how to speak, where to speak, and, more important, when to speak.

TWENTY

The False Sense of Entitlement

Utilized properly, the FBI's powerful law enforcement authority opens many doors for its investigators. That authority, however, does not infer special privileges to FBI agents or suggest that they are in some way better than other citizens. From their first day on the job, agents are taught that although they are "special agents," they cannot use their position or power in ways that would be, or could be, perceived as above the law.

The process for becoming an FBI agent is arduous, intense, and highly competitive. Besides meeting the FBI's basic educational, character, and fitness qualifications, along with a thorough background check, applicants must pass a slate of aptitude and psychological tests. If the interviews go well and the candidate possesses a particular skill that the FBI needs, he or she may become one of the small number of agents who are hired each year.

A new FBI agent spends four months of intensive and rigorous training at the FBI Academy, where, upon successfully graduating, he or she will take an oath to uphold and defend the Constitution and be given a badge and a gun. Each graduate understands that carrying the FBI badge automatically holds him or her to a higher standard of conduct than that of other citizens and that he or she must rise above any temptation to use that badge to obtain inappropriate favors or special privileges.

Over the years, a few agents have mistakenly believed that they deserved exceptional treatment from the public by virtue of their law enforcement status. Failing to live up to the higher standards and dishonoring the FBI have been catastrophic for most of those agents. However, a few, like "Dennis," have learned important lessons from early errors and managed to save their careers.

Dennis went through the same FBI selection and training process as his peers in the New York office. When he arrived from the Academy, where he had been taught about the specific authorities of FBI agents, Dennis was assigned to work with a senior agent. Together, the training agent and Dennis hunted down fugitives and bank robbers, gathered evidence, and built cases. For Dennis, and others like him, this was a perfect job and a way to learn a variety of investigative techniques from a competent veteran.

It takes a while for a new employee in the FBI subculture to become accepted by the group. One generally recognizes when this acceptance occurs because he or she is invited to participate in special activities and customs. For Dennis, being asked to go to lunch with his training agent and his training agent's friends signaled their recognition that he was "one of the guys." He was pleased that he had proven himself to his new peer group but tried to keep his satisfaction to himself.

At the group's favorite deli that day, one of the more senior agents took Dennis aside and told him that the owner loved the FBI and treated the agents especially well. "In fact," he told Dennis, "this guy makes the best roast beef sandwiches in the city. Just show him your badge and tell him if you want more and he'll load you up!"

This deal sounded good to Dennis, as there were few things better than a thick, New York deli sandwich. When it was his turn to order, Dennis asked the owner for a roast beef sandwich. As he had been told, he then held out his badge and quietly said, "FBI—more roast beef." To his surprise the aggravated owner looked at Dennis as if he were an alien from another planet. The other guys, watching and hearing this interaction, burst into laughter. Dennis saw that the joke was on him. They had succeeded in getting one over on the new guy. The deli owner apparently failed to find humor in the setup and handed Dennis a very ordinary roast beef sandwich.

The penalty for Dennis's transgression was an unforgettable moment of embarrassment that, fortunately, damaged only his ego. The reward for his action was actually a very valuable lesson from which Dennis learned that the only entitlement associated with the FBI badge is that of service. This small, unintentional misjudgment reminded Dennis of what he been taught about FBI agents maintaining a higher standard of behavior and how easy it could be for him to destroy the career for which he had worked so hard.

TOO IMPORTANT TO FAIL?

Mark Putnam arrived in the FBI's Miami office after completing his first Bureau assignment in Kentucky. Eager to start a new phase of his life, he took to his Florida assignment immediately and was always available when someone needed a backup. He continued to work on improving the investigative skills he had developed in Kentucky until his poor judgment and false sense of power caused him to lose everything.

Not long after Mark arrived in Miami, Jim Huggins, a supervisor in the Louisville office who had worked with Mark, called Bill Gavin, who was the SAC of the Miami office, with some disturbing news. Investigators from the Kentucky State Police (KSP) were looking into the mysterious disappearance of a woman named Susan Daniels Smith, and Mark Putnam had surfaced as a person of interest, although not a suspect. Bill directed two Miami office supervisors to interview Mark, who was married, about his relationship with the missing woman. Mark cooperated with the interviewers, but neither supervisor believed the story that he told them about their association.

As Huggins and the KSP continued to look for Ms. Smith, they discovered evidence indicating that Mark might have had an inappropriate relationship with her. Strangely, they also found out that Mark had recently rented a car in Louisville and returned it to the rental agency with a broken windshield.

At this point, a KSP investigator and FBI supervisor Huggins flew to Miami to interview him more fully. During this interview, Mark's story seemed even less credible than his earlier version had. Although Bill did not know Mark well at this point, his situation was so serious that Bill realized he needed to become more involved. Bill arranged to talk with Mark privately. As they spoke, Mark began to show physical signs of excessive concern over what was happening to him. Finally, Mark said that he wanted to talk with Bill but thought he should get an attorney first.

By now it seemed very likely that this FBI agent, who months earlier had been an up-and-coming law enforcement officer, was somehow involved in Susan Smith's disappearance. Bill helped Mark find an attorney, and Mark was able to discuss what had happened to Susan. Bill was deeply grieved by the story he told.

While in Kentucky, Mark had been one of the few agents assigned to the rural area of Pikeville. Being from urban Connecticut, he was much more familiar with city culture than with country ways, and he knew that he would need assistance and information from local residents to adequately identify and address the area's crime problems. Furthermore, FBI agents were expected to develop informants, or individuals who had knowledge about criminals and their activities. Mark knew that he would be regularly evaluated on his ability to find and connect with these informants.

Mark had an easy personal style and his prestigious position and personal attractiveness helped him to get to know Susan Smith and employ her as an informant. A native of the area, she knew nearly everyone in town and was able to introduce Mark to people he wanted to meet and to provide him with information that was helpful in conducting investigations.

Like a big fish in a little pond, Mark was living large and began to believe that he was, indeed, someone special. As time went on, Mark and Susan's relationship became intimate. Although Mark's supervisor was unaware of the affair, Mark knew that this type of behavior was in violation of FBI rules and had to end. When the news of Mark's transfer to Miami arrived, he thought he had found a simple way out of the capricious relationship. Instead of saying her good-byes, however, Susan informed Mark that she was pregnant with his child. Now, the high esteem that Mark had enjoyed because of his status as an FBI agent rang hollow. He had to find a way to resolve this problem without destroying his family and his career.

After being transferred to Miami, Mark had traveled back to Kentucky in order to meet with Susan and resolve the issue of her pregnancy. He picked her up in his rental car and drove to a remote, wooded area to discuss the problem. Mark told Susan that she should have an abortion, but she refused and demanded that he leave his family to be with her and their unborn baby. When Mark made it clear he would not do as she asked, Susan threatened to go public with their affair and her pregnancy. Emotions running high, Mark and Susan began to fight physically. As she was defending herself, she kicked out the car's windshield. Finally, in a fit of rage and despair Mark strangled the woman who had been his secret lover.

At the time Mark confessed to murdering Susan, investigators had not yet found her remains. As part of his plea agreement, Mark agreed to direct them to the place where he had hidden her body. Based on his instructions, searchers discovered her body lying in a ravine that, ironically, was scheduled to be flooded and converted into a lake, and it might have prevented her from ever being found. Locating Susan brought closure, but not comfort, to her family and a sixteen-year prison sentence for Mark Putnam.

FBI agents are often treated with deference by the public, but no one is entitled to violate the law—even to protect the reputation of the Bureau. This case was the only time an FBI agent has ever been convicted of such a horrific crime, and Mark's failure to live up to the law and the high personal standards of the FBI devastated his wife and his children and affected the entire Bureau family. Sadly, his promising future was destroyed by his hubris, foolishness, and immaturity.

There is, of course, a significant difference between asking for a free meal and taking someone's life. But developing a false sense of entitlement can be an occupational risk for all executives, especially those who are treated like organizational royalty. Professionals who find themselves in a situation calling for an ethical decision, as most eventually will, need a strong moral grounding to enable them to choose the correct and unpretentious course of action.

- Regardless of their size or mission, organizations need core values that are translated into policies and communicated regularly to their employees.
- The behavior of the ethically grounded leader becomes the model for his or her employees.
- Leaders should be alert for behaviors and attitudes in their employees—or in themselves—that signal the presence or the possibility of a false sense of entitlement.

TWENTY-ONE

The Root of (Nearly) Every Problem

Ineffective communication is the root of many interpersonal and organizational problems. Whether communication is nonexistent, poorly conveyed, or imprudent, it can negatively impact the performance of the organization and place unnecessary pressure on its leaders. Lack of communication can also cause an employee undue concern and stress. A misunderstood comment can create a misperception of intent, and an ill-timed or public remark can negatively impact a career.

A few years ago, an FBI manager gave a speech to a large audience that comprised mainly on-duty and former military officers. The topic was how to identify procurement fraud, waste, and abuse in the defense industry. The manager had recently read some criticism of military spending in a well-known national magazine and decided to incorporate some of the author's opinions in the speech.

After the manager's remarks, a member of the audience came up to the speaker and tactfully pointed out that he and some other attendees had been insulted by one of the statements that the manager had made in his speech. Although the manager was merely restating the opinion of the author of the article he had read, it was interpreted by the audience as his opinion. The manager regretted what he had done and knew there was no way to undo the damage he had caused except to apologize. He realized he should have run a draft of the speech by a colleague for feedback.

The manager's inadequate preparation for the presentation had three unintended, negative results: a gathering of good public servants had been criticized publicly, the manager had embarrassed himself for his inability to understand the potential impact of his words, and, most of all, the FBI's reputation had been diminished because, at that place and time, the manager was the face and voice of the FBI.

TELL ME WHAT I NEED TO KNOW

In her first few months as an FBI agent in San Francisco, Kathleen McChesney was assigned to several different squads to gain a better understanding of the breadth of the Bureau's investigative responsibilities. The supervisor of each squad had a unique management style and much could be learned from watching the way with which the cases and her fellow employees were dealt.

Most of Kathleen's coworkers were friendly and helpful, taking the time to show her and other new agents how to prepare reports, conduct record checks, and, most important, find the keys to the government cars. The other agents on the squad were also a key source of information, passing on news about cases and gossiping among themselves, which occasionally blurred the lines between fact and fiction. This was very different from Kathleen's experience on the King County police force in Washington, where daily roll calls and bulletins provided officers and detectives with the information they needed for their shifts or investigations. If anyone conveyed incorrect information, that person was responsible for correcting it.

One of Kathleen's earliest assignments was to a squad responsible for investigating organized crime cases. Once again, Kathleen looked to her squad mates for the information that she needed to do her job and stay out of harm's way. The squad did not have a permanent supervisor, but Bruce Gebhardt, a young agent who had recently transferred to San Francisco from Denver, was functioning in the role of acting supervisor.

The acting supervisor program is one of the FBI's most effective leadership and management training techniques. Agents are given the opportunity—for several weeks or months—to function as the supervisor of a squad of agents, making decisions, leading raids, and dealing with executive management on behalf of a squad. The acting supervisor is expected to make all of the work assignments, to provide the agents with the resources they need to do their jobs, and to evaluate the work product of each individual squad member. Acting supervisors are also evaluated by their superiors to determine if they have the right skills, instincts, and leadership ability for promotion to a permanent supervisor position. The program not only weeds out many of those who have difficulty leading, it provides a realistic experience for the agents so that they can determine whether they can cope with the myriad, non-investigative issues that a supervisor must address each day.

A few jokesters tried to test Kathleen by warning her that an acting supervisor wasn't a "real" supervisor and that if the acting supervisor ever made a decision or gave agents a directive that they did not agree with, that the agents could ignore it or appeal to a higher level of management without fear of reprisal. Fortunately Kathleen didn't adopt that particular way of thinking but did observe that once a peer became an acting supervisor, he or she was the frequent topic of conversation among the squad members. Each well-intended or ill-advised action or remark made by the acting supervisor could generate endless hours of criticism.

During Kathleen's first week on the organized crime squad, Bruce called a squad meeting. Unlike other squad meetings she had attended that seemed to be a waste of time, the meeting Bruce conducted was actually informative and useful. He was obviously prepared and referred to his notes periodically as he succinctly described the major issues that were going on in the FBI, the San Francisco office, and the squad. He pointed out future training opportunities, went through a calendar of important events, and then asked the squad members to briefly update everyone on the status of their most important cases.

Within thirty-five minutes of this well-structured meeting, Kathleen learned more about what was going on in the FBI and the San Francisco office than she had in the previous three months. She later observed that many other effective FBI leaders used this simple process when there were important matters to communicate, and they avoided wasting everyone's time and energy when there were not.

TELL ME NOW, NOT LATER

The FBI's Chicago office is its fourth largest, with a rich history of some of the Bureau's most famous gangster cases—think John Dillinger and Baby Face Nelson—and a strong reputation for battling corruption and organized crime. Before Kathleen arrived in Chicago as the SAC, she talked many times with her predecessor, Larry Collins. Larry shared with her his perspectives on the office's ongoing investigations and the relationships between the FBI and the other law enforcement agencies. In preparation for her taking over Larry's role, they also discussed the quality of the personnel, the adequacy of the financial resources, and the employees' working conditions.

An FBI leader will sometimes begin a project only to be transferred elsewhere, leaving behind unfulfilled promises and disappointed employees. Kathleen asked Larry if there was any business that he felt was unfinished, so she could complete the work for him. Without hesitation, Larry said that he had hoped to find better office space for the employees but that neither FBI Headquarters nor the federal government's landlord, the General Services Administration (GSA), was willing to approve a new building or office relocation. Larry had been able to secure and refurbish some additional office space, but, with more than eight hundred people assigned to the FBI office, this was only a stopgap measure. Soon even this annex would be crowded.

On Kathleen's first day in the Chicago FBI office, she toured the space with the senior office managers. The Everett M. Dirksen Federal Building, which housed the FBI office, had been built long before the 1995 bombing of the Murrah Federal Office Building in Oklahoma City. Therefore, many of its security measures had been added on, rather than built into, its infrastructure. The original builders had not envisioned Internet access cables, and the subfloors and dropped ceilings were a complicated mess of wires and cords. By far, this was the most cramped and cluttered FBI office space she had seen, and she could easily understand why Larry strongly urged her to find a way to help the employees get out of this controlled chaos.

As she met with different groups of employees around the office during the next few weeks, Kathleen promised to find a way to help them find better workspace. Everyone was polite, but their facial expressions and body language told her that they were skeptical that anything would be done.

Kathleen asked the office manager to survey the employees and gather their recommendations for possible locations for a new office. A representative group of employees was assembled to provide opinions on the project and to relay progress reports back to their coworkers. Information about the evolving plan was included in the office's monthly newsletter, discussed at nearly every management and employee meeting, and sketches of other FBI offices' building projects were posted on the bulletin boards. With this much information being shared, it seemed as if every base was covered.

It took more than a year of meetings, briefings, and visits to FBI Headquarters and other federal officials to obtain approval from the GSA to move the entire FBI office into its own space. The next step was to a find a location that would meet the unique requirements of the FBI, the GSA, and the city of Chicago. One snowy December morning, Kathleen and the executive management team went to look at the possible sites for the new office. As luck would have it, there was vacant land in an area being redeveloped west of downtown Chicago that was available for a good price. The team became more enthusiastic about the area as they drove up and down the slushy streets and finally agreed to ask the GSA to relocate the FBI offices to this property.

Later that day Kathleen learned that some of the employees were angry about not being told that a decision had just been made about the new location. By not making a timely announcement about such an important project, rumors began to fly around the office, and many anxious employees wanted to know what was going on. At her office manager's wise suggestion, Kathleen promptly called a meeting with the concerned coworkers. A discussion with worried, unhappy employees did not sound like much fun, but it had to be done. Kathleen held the meeting knowing that, as a leader, it would be impossible to please everyone. Nonetheless, the discussion helped to correct some misperceptions about the move and, happily, sparked some new enthusiasm for the project. Over the next five years, the project managers and dozens of other FBI employees embraced the work that needed to be done. As good leaders do, they tried their best to create an environment in which every employee would be proud to work. The result of their efforts was the construction of the largest stand-alone FBI office in the country—a structure that is now a model for Bureau operations nationwide.

Not every leader will have to deal with a major relocation or renovation or building a new building. However, every leader and manager should learn the dos and don'ts of changing an employee's work space. Whether the project involves putting someone's desk closer to the window or moving the entire office to another state, contentious issues will arise. People naturally become comfortable and secure in their spaces and generally protest even the smallest change. Dissatisfied employees will convey their distress to their coworkers

and supervisors as they attempt to retain the status quo. The bigger the relocation project is, the more often the person in charge will have to arbitrate
conflicts ranging from petty to significant.

Knowing when and how to keep your employees apprised of important
matters that may affect them may be more of an art than a science, but un-
ambiguous communication is essential to a well-functioning organization. A
carefully crafted and delivered message can help employees better understand
and complete their work and even prompt them to become more integrated
and productive.

I KNOW WHAT I SAID, BUT THAT'S NOT WHAT I MEANT

Our colleague "Geoff" was a very successful fugitive hunter, and in his first
dozen years in the FBI, he developed a reputation for hard work and high energy. He "paid his dues" for a promotion by accepting a transfer to FBI Headquarters and spending two years managing new investigative programs in the
Criminal Division. As his tour of duty in Washington was about to end, Geoff
applied to become the supervisor of one of the FBI's more desirable satellite
offices in the southeastern United States. After he landed the plum assignment, he spent several days learning all that he could about the new office and
community so that he would become the best leader that he could possibly be.

On his first day on the new job, Geoff called his employees together to
speak to them as a group. He told them about investigations he had conducted, hoping to gain their immediate confidence in his leadership ability. He
also described his work at FBI Headquarters and talked about his expectations
for the office. Geoff thought the short meeting was going well, and as he concluded his remarks he made an attempt to energize his new team.

"I know you have had other supervisors who haven't stayed here very
long," he said. "I am not one of those guys. I want you to know that I plan
to retire right here."

The senior agents in the office were pleased that Geoff recognized the
importance of continuity of leadership. Based on his comments, it seemed
clear that he was not going to act as some of their previous managers had and
drop in from FBI Headquarters to warm up a seat before catching the next
promotion and moving on. Geoff was possibly the "real deal"—a supervisor

who would spend his time guiding and championing their work rather than looking for ways to obtain another promotion.

On the other hand, the newer agents were baffled. As they talked among themselves, they wondered why someone, especially a new supervisor, would point out his lack of ambition by saying that he had come to the office to retire. How could they continue to be enthusiastic and excited about their work when their own boss was focused on his life after the FBI? Unlike the senior agents who were happy to meet Geoff, the younger agents were discouraged by their new leader's comments. They pegged him as disinterested and lazy.

Geoff did not realize his words had created a problem until he had a chance meeting with a former mentor from FBI Headquarters some months later. The mentor, a down-to-earth and much-admired executive, had heard that Geoff had not made an entirely smooth transition to his new assignment. During their conversation, the mentor listened carefully as Geoff enthusiastically described some of the cases his employees were investigating. Geoff even seemed highly motivated to become a good mentor himself.

"I sure am glad to hear you have a lot of good things going in that office," his mentor said. "But you know, word's gotten back that you just took that job so that you could get a head start on your retirement. Some of your new folks are thinking that you've lost your passion for the job. You might have to correct some wrong assumptions."

Geoff was stunned to hear that any of his subordinates thought he might be disinterested in them or their work. To the contrary, even though he was now a supervisor, he loved to do agent's work and was truly committed to the FBI and his employees. He remembered his well-intentioned remark about planning to stay in his job until he retired and felt certain that the senior agents fully understood what he meant. Apparently, those same words conveyed an entirely different message to the younger agents who now had a poor and inaccurate impression of him.

"That's totally off the mark," Geoff explained. "I wanted everyone to know that I planned to serve them as their leader, that I wouldn't start to build relationships with them and then jump ship for a better job somewhere else in the Bureau or to retire. I thought I was letting them know I would be loyal to them. What can I do to fix this?"

"That's easy," his mentor said. "Go back and tell 'em what you thought you told 'em."

- Understand and exploit the power of an accurate, timely, and clear message.
- Communicate regularly and effectively to motivate and inspire, as well as to direct and inform.
- Develop and maintain strong communication skills, especially the ability to listen carefully and considerately to your colleagues.

TWENTY-TWO

When the Pursuit of Perfection Impedes Progress

Known throughout the FBI as one of its finest investigators, "Roger" was consistently asked to travel around the country and work on the Bureau's most complex and sensitive cases. He was thorough and organized, and he understood emerging technologies and how their use could help to solve cases. He was also uniquely creative and often came up with valuable new ideas to apply to investigations or administrative processes.

Although the best investigators do not always become good leaders, Roger's boss knew that he was uniquely talented. If he became a supervisor, Roger would surely help his employees improve their detective skills and would make certain that no one "left a stone unturned" when it came to their case work. With a push from his superiors, Roger was easily promoted to his first management position.

Over time Roger moved up to positions of greater responsibility. He was recognized and admired for his tenacity and focus on the mission, and he was especially good at making sure his team members were rewarded for their accomplishments. He also encouraged the more capable men and women to seek promotion, perhaps believing that "Roger-trained" managers would improve the FBI's cadre of leaders.

Roger excelled at management, just as he had at investigations. He was considered to be an exceptional leader—up to a point. Roger had four hyper-management traits that consistently frustrated his employees: occasionally assigning the identical task or project to different agents, repeatedly returning a work product for insignificant changes, delegating non-priority work to employees who were already overassigned, and excessively overseeing and following up on assignments.

Generally agents would not be aware that Roger had tasked them to do something he had already asked another to do. As the projects were completed, Roger would compare the results and, often, create a third work product that he would send back to one of the agents for additional work. It took longer for some employees to catch on to Roger's method of operation and even longer for someone to confront him about it.

One subordinate spent hours gathering information on a project for Roger, only to find out that one of his peers had been contacting the same sources. The agent called Roger and asked him why he was doing the identical tasks as his peer. Roger candidly said that he liked to see competition among his employees and wanted to find out which agent would complete the work first and who would produce a better product. This particular approach might be helpful in certain fields, but with limited resources and grave and exigent matters to deal with, an FBI agent's time cannot be wasted, especially when there was little discernible difference in the abilities of the agents.

Roger delegated a number of routine duties to his subordinates that helped them improve their management skills. It also gave him time to read every document produced by his subordinates and make suggestions for writing a better report or memorandum. In most cases, the original works were sufficient, but Roger consistently sought perfection. He would often add or change words and paragraphs and return documents to the employee for a "re-do." His pursuit of perfection slowed down the process, was inefficient, and, unfortunately, caused some employees to lose confidence in their abilities or to lose interest in creating a great product the first time, knowing their work would have to be changed anyway to suit the boss's whim.

The ingenuity that Roger displayed in conducting his own investigations was one of the skills that had helped him to become highly successful in his career. Whether he was driving, having lunch, or working out, he was constantly conjuring up new projects. Roger believed that all ideas needed to be explored, and he would task his employees with evaluating the new concepts regardless of their priority or importance. Unfortunately, these men and women were usually overburdened with other assignments that Roger should have considered before piling on the new work.

Even after years of management experience, Roger inaccurately believed that everyone could, and should, perform certain tasks as quickly as he could. Though project follow-up is important, Roger would begin to nag his employees to finish their work long before it was expected or could reasonably be completed. One subordinate tells of a meeting in Roger's office where he was given an assignment and before he returned to his own office Roger had called to see if it was completed. Another joked that Roger expected assignments to be completed even before he had even thought of them.

To his credit, Roger's hyper-management traits frequently helped his employees improve their skills. His idiosyncrasies, on the other hand, could be discouraging and morale crushing. Unfortunately, like Roger, some bosses may never be able to recognize the point at which the pursuit of perfection impedes progress.

- If the leader holds the team back, the team may lose the desire to move forward.
- Refrain from overwhelming your team members with unrealistic deadlines or objectives.
- To encourage the group's best performance, draw out superior work and ideas from employees of all abilities and temperaments.

TWENTY-THREE

Too Tight on the Reins

A favorite of several FBI directors, "Carl" was as brilliant as he was ener-
getic and was an example of a tireless manager dedicated to the Bureau. After
spending a few years as an investigator, this quick-witted attorney transferred
to FBI Headquarters, where he impressed others with his ability to understand
the political minefields that the FBI must clear in order to maintain its credibility with the other agencies and all branches of government. As an adviser
to dozens of top-level executives, Carl was known for his ability to "read the
tea leaves" and to preempt an interagency conflict.

Rather than transferring to and from FBI Headquarters as most executives did, Carl stayed in Washington after his initial promotion. This allowed
him to gain a rare in-depth knowledge of the ways of "the Beltway" and to
develop long-term relationships with some of government's most powerful
leaders. Although he had a nontraditional career path and his roles required
that he only manage a small number of employees, Carl's value to the organization continued to grow.

Carl's strong work ethic was matched by the men and women he selected
to work with him. Often involved in the FBI's major incidents and issues,
Carl's team members could be found making calls, writing reports, and working on projects at all hours. Despite their talents and dedication, however, Carl
reviewed every aspect of the work produced by his handpicked employees and
kept them out of the internal limelight that could highlight their special abilities to his superiors.

Teaching his employees how to do their jobs came naturally to Carl, and he never neglected to provide them with the resources that they needed for their work. While those actions were important, he never showed any of his subordinates how to do his job and restricted their training opportunities to what he personally provided. Consequently, it became very difficult for his team members to develop professionally.

It was also hard for some of Carl's employees to understand why he failed to mentor them or recognize when their responsibilities began to significantly exceed those for which they were being compensated. Some wondered if it was because Carl had limited experience in directly supervising employees. Others thought he was afraid that his subordinate's abilities might outshine his and that he would be replaced. Curiously, when another manager asked him what he planned to do to recognize the additional work his employees were handling, Carl said that he was deliberately doing nothing so that the director would not think that he was trying to "build an empire."

When Carl finally retired from the FBI, his successor immediately recognized that Carl's inattention to his employees' professional development had caused the careers of some very capable men and women to stagnate. Some of Carl's more talented employees had become discouraged by his micromanagement style and moved on to other jobs. Furthermore, Carl's unwillingness to ask the director for additional employees or to secure just compensation for his overworked staff at the risk of appearing greedy was unfair to his team. Carl's replacement easily convinced the director to increase his staff and raise its members' pay levels. To no one's surprise, Carl's replacement was never accused of empire building.

- Maintain reasonable workloads and appropriate salary levels for your employees to keep them motivated and optimistic.
- Help your subordinates develop professionally, even at the risk of losing them for better opportunities.
- Teach your employees how to do your job, and be grateful when someone does it better than you do.
- Redirect the light that shines on you as the leader to showcase the special abilities of your team.

PART IV

PROMOTION OBSESSION

The FBI's organizational structure may best be described as a lumpy pyramid. Sprinkled throughout this pyramid are hundreds of informal leaders, or men and women who are role models for their coworkers through their actions and values. The formal leaders are fewer in number but more recognizable by their titles and authority. The path to these more visible leadership positions is well stated in FBI policies, although there are times that someone with a unique skill or experience can fly past the competition on the way to the top.

We often mistakenly think that being assigned to supervise coworkers is validation of our importance to the organization, much like the child who is put in charge of siblings when his or her parents are away. American business culture reinforces the perception that the men and women at the highest levels of the organization are its most important assets because they are paid higher salaries and have more attractive work environments than the other employees. The enhanced status of the leader sometimes becomes an end unto itself, and many employees who would otherwise be quite content to forgo the added responsibilities of management find themselves competing for leadership positions that they don't really want or understand. Social and family pressure to get ahead and to be the boss and the belief in a mythical right to be promoted drive some very unqualified employees to constantly chase after higher-level positions in humorous, demeaning, and, sometimes, sad ways.

Once they have reached a position of leadership, some men and women mistakenly believe they are the office and require all of its trappings to build and maintain their self-confidence. These individuals are generally unwilling to share the limelight with their subordinates. To the detriment of their organization and their employees, these egocentric characters "live well beyond their shadows."

TWENTY-FOUR

Am I in the Package?

Being selected for a management position in the FBI can be the beginning of a meteoric rise to the Bureau's highest executive levels and an enormous ego boost. For some men and women, a promotion is merely a means to an end—a transfer to a more interesting or challenging job or a chance to relocate to a more desirable city or state. The majority of altruistic, confident agents, however, finds that taking on management responsibility allows them to mentor and teach subordinates to become successful investigators. As they become good supervisors and even better leaders, each one plays a part in making the FBI a better organization and in sustaining its remarkable reputation.

An exclusive group of FBI executives belong to the mid-level and senior executive career boards. The boards are responsible for selecting and promoting the candidates for routine promotions and for recommending a slate of candidates, referred to as "the package," for the Bureau's highest-level and internationally based positions. The package, usually consisting of the names and main qualifications of three or four candidates, is provided to the FBI director for a final selection.

If a candidate is fortunate enough to be friendly with a board member, the member might serve as the candidate's "hook" and speak up for him or her during a selection meeting. However, if a board member does not like a candidate, it is quite possible that he or she will "tube" the candidate by speaking against the agent during deliberations. The majority of agents competing for promotions do not have any hooks or know any career board members personally, although some have tried to befriend them in some very amusing ways. A few, like "Dan," "Rick," and "Kurt," were obsessed with being promoted in ways that came to define their professional personas. Their actions and behaviors illustrate some of the more disheartening aspects of competition, organizational politics, and human nature.

IT'S NOT WHO YOU KNOW—IT'S WHO KNOWS YOU!

Dan was at the very top of the "eager-to-be-promoted" scale. This young man had spent a few years assigned to a field office, investigating criminal cases, but he hadn't really impressed anyone with his results. Having a title, more pay, and the little prestige that went with a supervisory position meant everything to him, so when entry-level management positions became vacant at FBI Headquarters, Dan applied for all of them. After a fair number of attempts, Dan was selected for one of the jobs and got his desired promotion and transfer to Washington.

Although he had garnered this one promotion despite a mediocre work record, Dan did not seem to understand the relationship between outstanding performance and the ability to achieve that next promotion. On the very day he arrived at headquarters, he started planning his next move up the career ladder. He spent endless hours annoying his coworkers by talking incessantly about promotions—time that would have been better spent developing his management and interpersonal skills.

When Dan began applying for his next promotion, he failed to consider that his lackluster performance might hold him back. Despite his professional limitations, he began to compete for several new jobs every week. The career board members, however, did not believe Dan was qualified for that next step up the career ladder and never seriously considered him for further promotion. Knowing that his fate was in the hands of those who were repeatedly rejecting him, Dan decided to find a way to meet every member of the career board. He was hopeful, though mistaken, that once those executives met him they would surely select him for a plum job.

Dan's mission to make himself known to the career board members began by his locating each of their offices in the FBI Headquarters building. He then talked with anyone who might know a board member and gathered information about the schedules they kept, when they went to lunch, and if they worked out. Deciding that a happenstance meeting with a board member in the Bureau's gym might be his best bet, Dan began to coordinate his own workout times with those of board members who used the facility. Since Dan never missed a daily workout, his chances of making at least one self-introduction were pretty good.

One day Dan got the timing right and succeeded in meeting his first career board member. He was very pleased that he had managed to have a short conversation with one of his "targets" and became even more eager for another. Dan decided to start going to the gym twice a day.

At the time Dan was trying to win his next promotion, Kathleen and her partner Rob Grace were managing the FBI's career development program at FBI Headquarters. One afternoon Rob came back to the office from the gym looking very amused. He told Kathleen that when he had gone to the men's locker room to get ready for a noon basketball game, Dan had just finished a workout and was heading back to his office. An hour later, after Rob had finished his game and was leaving the locker room, he was surprised to see Dan returning to the gym.

Rob chided him. "Hey, Dan, didn't I just see you leave here a while ago?"

Dan explained, "Yeah, but see, I found out this is a great way to meet these career board guys, and since they work out at different times, I need to get down here more than once a day."

When Rob finished laughing, he said, "Look, son, I think you might be better off going back to work right now. Besides, you'll be working all evening if you start spending most of your day down here. And don't you suppose that your supervisor is going to notice your extended absences?"

After that encounter with Dan, Rob and Kathleen spent a considerable amount of time counseling him. Dan eventually realized that he lacked the skills, and even the real desire, to supervise an investigative squad. He finally gave up his quest for a bigger title and returned to an investigative position in a field office near his hometown, where he likely never missed a workout.

SEE ME, PROMOTE ME!

Like Dan, Rick was passionate about his career and a chance to be the SAC of a field office. There are fewer than a hundred of these coveted positions in the FBI, and many consider being selected for one to be the pinnacle of an agent's management career.

Rick had done his homework on the senior executive career board and its members. He knew that this career board did not select SACs; rather, they created the "package" for every SAC opening. He was confident that he would be included in some of the SAC packages as he knew all of the career board members and even considered a few to be good friends. Rick also knew that it was the FBI director who would ultimately select or reject him for promotion and that he needed a strategy to become a SAC.

To game this correctly, Rick believed he had to establish a better relationship with the director or, at the very least, have some significant face time with him. Unfortunately for Rick, his current assignment rarely brought him into contact with the director, so he came up with an amusing way to make certain that he and the director had more frequent personal contact.

Rick's plan to run into the director was discovered accidentally by "Steve," one of his friends at headquarters. One of Steve's responsibilities was to brief the FBI director several times a week regarding interagency issues. On his way to one of these briefings, he saw Rick loitering near the water fountain outside the director's door. Steve noticed that each time the door opened, Rick bent down to take a drink. He thought Rick's behavior might have been a fluke until he saw him in the same place the following week. There was Rick, bobbing up and down at the water fountain like a duck, waiting for that special moment when he could "unexpectedly" have a conversation with the only man who could appoint him to his dream job.

Steve was merciless when he told Rick he had discovered his plan. To make matters worse, he revealed Rick's juvenile plot to a group of their friends. Of course, Rick denied the scheme, but he did start using another drinking fountain closer to his own office.

WHEN HARD WORK IS NOT ENOUGH

One day an FBI employee "Mary" came to see Kathleen about her husband, Kurt, a fellow FBI employee. Mary was quite concerned that Kurt was becoming depressed because he had not been able to secure his next promotion, and many of his peers had started to surpass him on the career ladder. Kathleen reminded Mary that she could not discuss Kurt's situation with her but suggested that Kurt himself might want to schedule a career counseling session with her or Rob.

Apparently Kurt's career progress was a frequent topic at home (and quite possibly of more importance to Kurt's wife than to him) because the very next day Kurt called for a career guidance appointment. Rob and Kathleen were well aware that Kurt had applied for dozens of jobs, but he had never been competitive or even in the package of candidates proposed for promotion. During his counseling session, Kathleen asked Kurt why he thought his job applications weren't being seriously considered. Kurt said he couldn't think of any negatives that could be impacting his ability to compete for a higher-level assignment. Turning the question around, Rob asked him why he believed he was a better candidate than those who had surpassed him in competition.

"I work hard. I have years of experience. I have done everything the FBI has asked me to do," he responded.

"I guess you think that's enough?" Rob asked.

Kurt snapped back, "Well, it should be."

In their previous deliberations about Kurt, the members of the career board had recognized that the things Kurt said about himself were true—he was a hard worker who never refused an assignment, no matter how difficult or time consuming. But it was also true that that no board member found Kurt friendly or enjoyable to be around.

"Look, Kurt," Kathleen tried to explain, "while being promoted isn't a popularity contest, it kind of is. How many friends do you have in the FBI?"

The man looked stunned. "What do you mean?"

"I mean friends," she said. "Who do you like to spend time with? Who likes to spend time with you? Who do you eat lunch with? When's the last time you shared a cup of coffee or went to the gym with a coworker?"

Still bewildered, Kurt asked, "Are you telling me I have to have friends to get the job I have earned—the job I deserve?"

"No, we are telling you that if you can't find ways to relate to people, you shouldn't be hoping to lead them," Rob said firmly.

"Well," he said, "does the career board think that way too?"

"Probably. By the way, when's the last time you smiled or said anything nice to anyone?" Kathleen asked.

Kurt, scowling as usual, just shrugged. He had put all his emotional energy into his family and his work, but none into his FBI associates. Although he had a kind heart, there was a bridge a mile wide between him and his peers.

It was important that Kurt understand this point if he was going to move up any further in the FBI. "It's not that people dislike you, Kurt. It's that they haven't found anything about you to like, either. We don't want bosses that we can't get to know or like as a person."

"Well, they don't have to like me," he said. "They just have to respect me."

Technically, Kurt was correct in his assessment of the situation, but as bright as he was, he was not absorbing the message about his lack of interpersonal skills. Rob arranged for Kurt to meet with two well-liked senior supervisors who provided him with some excellent advice about relating to coworkers in a positive way. One even directed Kurt to look at himself in the mirror and practice smiling.

After a noticeable effort to be friendlier and submitting several more applications for promotion, Kurt finally achieved his goal and was transferred to an FBI field office on the West Coast. His new employees thought well of him for his work ethic and knowledge about investigations, but, sadly, no one ever called him a friend.

Dan believed that the selection process was all about politics, Rick thought that being seen by the FBI director would lead to his appointment as the head of an FBI office, and Kurt was convinced that his accomplishments were all that mattered in furthering his career. Each of these men were partially right in their assessment of the FBI's promotion process—that is, that it is necessary to establish a record of hard work and achievement and that it is helpful to have influential persons know you and observe you in a positive light. These individuals were so obsessed with being promoted, however, that their behavior made them caricatures, and their quest for a higher leadership role became much more difficult.

- Model yourself after the most respected executives in your organization to increase your chance to earn the privilege of leadership.
- Carefully assess your outward efforts to seek promotion and make sure that they are balanced, rational, and modest.
- As a leader, you have the responsibility to see that the executive development and promotion systems in your organization are fair and effective.

TWENTY-FIVE

Off to a Bad Start

A common way for FBI leaders to begin a new executive assignment is to gather everyone together for an "all employees" meeting. At these meetings the leader typically recognizes the mission, abilities, and recent activities of the staff. They might also describe their own prior FBI experiences and convey their goals and expectations for the office. Most of all, the best leaders will use this opportunity to assure the employees that they are proud of becoming a part of the office and the community and to begin to build strong bonds between themselves and their subordinates.

Most FBI leaders recognize the importance of being respectful to their new employees and of their cultural environment. Occasionally there are individuals like "Jerry" who missed this lesson, to the detriment of their coworkers and, ultimately, to the detriment of their own professional reputations.

"Jerry" spent a considerable amount of time in the cafeteria at FBI Headquarters talking with anyone who might be able to help him get promoted. Jerry's abilities were average at best, and his peers thought he should be happy with whatever assignment he received. His obsession and greatest mission was to transfer from FBI Headquarters and become the SAC of an FBI office in a Southern city, particularly one with a low cost of living.

After numerous unsuccessful applications to positions in locations that he found attractive, Jerry became frustrated. He told his superiors that he would now take any SAC assignment in order to get out of Washington. When the head of a northeastern field office announced his retirement, Jerry talked with his peers about applying for the position but ultimately decided against it. To his surprise, the director selected him for that job anyway.

Disappointed and pouting, Jerry asked to see the director in hopes of making an appeal for a different assignment. The director declined to meet with Jerry, referring him instead to his second in command, the deputy director. Jerry knew the deputy director couldn't rescind his transfer orders, so he didn't bother talking with him. Instead, like a spoiled child, he complained about his "raw deal" to anyone who would listen.

FBI policy provides agents a maximum of ninety days to move to a new location, although most SACs transfer in much less time. A few days before his ninety-day deadline, Jerry still had not made plans to move his family to the northeast or even rented a place to live. By then it was also well known that Jerry had not yet contacted his new secretary or any members of his future staff.

Around this time, the deputy director noticed that Jerry had not packed his personal items or moved one thing out of his office. Apparently Jerry still held out hope that something better might come along. On the eighty-ninth day, the deputy director walked into Jerry's office. Not one to mince words, he sternly and succinctly delivered his message: "Jerry, get the hell out of here."

A few "hall watchers" saw a disgusted deputy director leave Jerry's office that afternoon and hung around to see what Jerry would do next. Within a few minutes, Jerry came out of his office and walked slowly down to the copy room. He picked up some empty cardboard boxes and brought them back to his office to pack up his belongings and leave. By the ninetieth day, he was gone.

When Jerry finally arrived in his new office, the employees there were already well aware of his disinterest in his new assignment. Nonetheless, they were very curious to hear what he would say at his first all employees meeting. When that meeting began, Jerry's new deputy, the assistant special agent in charge (ASAC), introduced him to the crowd. As Jerry began to speak, a few were surprised at his candor, and everyone was surprised at his ignorance.

"I want you to know that I did not want to come here," Jerry said. "My family wanted to move down south, but the folks at FBI Headquarters didn't care anything about that. So here I am. I don't know how long I will be here, but I am looking to leave as soon as I can."

And then Jerry quickly turned and walked, alone, back to his new office.

A few months later, Jerry decided to retire from the FBI. The employees in his office were ecstatic. During his short time as their leader, he had done nothing to help them or to acknowledge the work of the office. Had he not chosen to leave when he did, the deputy director was prepared to remove Jerry from his prestigious position—the very role that he had worked for and then dishonored because it did not meet his personal criteria for happiness.

IF YOU CAN'T SAY SOMETHING NICE . . .

Another colleague "Tad" was a smart, witty, and generally upbeat manager who had a bright future in the FBI—that is, until he was transferred to an office in a small community that he found undesirable. Despite his new title and considerable responsibilities, he viewed his new assignment beneath his abilities and the community to be backward and undesirable. It didn't matter to Tad that the local area had good schools, a low crime rate, and friendly neighborhoods. He clearly thought of himself as a big-city kind of guy.

Instead of keeping his discontentment to himself, Tad occasionally spoke disparagingly about the community to his employees and members of the public. Both groups were proud of their culture and resented Tad's demeaning remarks. Tad took his criticism too far one day when he berated the citizens of the area at a civic event. A newspaper reporter happened to be in the audience and later asked the FBI director William Sessions what he thought of Tad's comments.

Director Sessions was a gentleman, well known for his courteous manner and consideration for all individuals and types of cultures. He did not tolerate disparaging remarks from any employee, and executives such as Tad were no exception. The director had some private words with Tad and later discussed the matter with senior executives. Although he didn't share the substance of the discussion he had with Tad, it was obvious that the director was quite upset about what had occurred. He conveyed his strong beliefs about the importance of becoming part of the community you serve and of honoring the people who live there. He then ordered his senior executives to reemphasize his message with the entire FBI leadership team.

While it was clear that Tad's comments had reflected poorly on himself and on the FBI, his greater mistake was to have failed to get to know his new employees and to try to understand, if not appreciate, their culture. It would have been beneficial for him, or for anyone transferring to a position in a new location, to have recognized that most people have strong, positive emotional attachments to their jobs and homes. Criticism directed at their work and life-styles, particularly from an authority figure, deflates morale and stifles the development of the important bond between the leader and his or her new team.

- Recognize the positive qualities and past accomplishments of your new employees in your initial dealings with them.
- When transferring to a new location, take the time to learn about your new employees, their work, and their community.
- To build solidarity and support in a new work environment, embrace some aspect of the culture or subculture in which you find yourself.
- Optimize your chances to make a good impression on new coworkers.

TWENTY-SIX

It's Not About You

FBI leaders are expected to have the requisite skills needed to guide agents who have been indirectly granted vast law enforcement powers by the Constitution, especially the authority to conduct investigations, make arrests, search and seize property, and, if necessary, use deadly force. To best use these skills, however, FBI leaders must be able to work with people in a sociable manner and to know that their most important responsibility is to serve those whom they are charged to lead.

One of Kathleen's favorite assignments in the FBI was as a supervisor in the Undercover and Sensitive Operations Unit at FBI Headquarters, part of the Criminal Investigative Division (CID). Each person in the unit was responsible for overseeing a part of the FBI's undercover program. The unit helped agents assigned to field offices throughout the country evaluate the use of the undercover technique in dealing with a crime problem in their territory, assisted them in developing and implementing realistic undercover scenarios, and selected and trained undercover operatives and managers. Providing this assistance as the undercover operations unfolded was fun and exciting, and the team established great working relationships with the agents running the cases, frequently resolving legal issues for them and connecting their undercover operation to a similar one in a different office for wider impact or security.

Not long after the FBI joined forces with the Drug Enforcement Administration to investigate illegal narcotics trafficking, Kathleen began to work with a group of agents from a southwestern office that was running an undercover operation against a cartel importing and selling heroin from Mexico and Southeast Asia. The enthusiastic FBI agents and a dozen local and state police officers were rapidly gathering significant evidence against dozens of suspects, and she was certain that this affable team was headed for success.

Every major undercover operation is required to undergo an on-site review by supervisors from the CID to confirm that the case is functioning according to its approved plan and to identify any particular needs or midcourse corrections that might need to be made. To conduct the on-site review of this particular operation, Kathleen and two other supervisors from headquarters traveled to the field office where it was being conducted and met the hardworking agents assigned to the case. The review group evaluated the progress of the undercover operation and recommended some additional techniques that might enhance the project. Although not everyone in a field office is happy to see people from headquarters, the services they provide are usually very welcome. In this case, the agents and police officers were grateful for the visit and made the most of the opportunity to showcase their investigation to the headquarters officials.

At the conclusion of each on-site review, the headquarters team presented its observations and recommendations during an "out briefing" with the field office's SAC. As they prepared to finish this particular assessment, the team joined the investigators and their supervisor in their SAC's office. Looking around the spacious room with its commanding view of the city, she noticed that every wall, from the chair rail to the ceiling, and every tabletop were covered with plaques, framed photographs, or newspaper articles bearing the SAC's name and/or likeness. She had never seen an office filled with as much personal memorabilia. She wondered how such a narcissist came to lead an FBI field office.

Kathleen and the other supervisors had many positive things to talk about with the SAC. They complimented the two agents who were responsible for the well-conceived operation and corresponding investigation. She asked the SAC if there was any additional assistance that headquarters might be able to provide.

The SAC seemed anxious to speak. He had been fidgeting during the briefing, and it appeared that he hadn't been listening to much of what had been said. Sitting up a little straighter in his chair, he looked directly at Kathleen. "Yes," he said sternly, "There is something else you can do! DON'T EVER CALL MY AGENTS AGAIN! You will call ME, and only ME, if you want to discuss this case!"

This spontaneous outburst caught everyone off guard. Either the man was unaware of how the positive relationship between his agents and the managers from headquarters had benefited the undercover operation, or he was choosing to ignore this partnership on behalf of his ego. He clearly hoped to control the access and information flow between FBI Headquarters and the agents assigned to his office. It was hard to imagine that he did not understand the impracticality of the headquarters team calling him every time it was necessary to convey information to his subordinates.

The SAC was obviously a person who loved to be in charge of everything, even at the risk of inefficiency and dysfunction. This man's sense of self-importance filled the room, suffocating everyone's energy and enthusiasm, and a hasty exit seemed prudent. As good-byes were said in front of his very embarrassed subordinates, it occurred to Kathleen that although the man had an ego the size of a small city, the level of his self-esteem was quite likely at the low end of the spectrum. Perhaps, instead of help, he needed understanding and pity, but as a result of that encounter no one was able to conjure up even the smallest amount of compassion for him.

The FBI would not be the effective and much admired agency it is if very many of its leaders were of this ilk. Unfortunately, similar managers are found in all types of organizations. As they wreak their own kind of self-centered havoc on their subordinates, they communicate their insecurities through their extreme behavior. A few of these flawed characters managed to find their way into the Bureau's leadership positions, creating difficulties for their respective superiors and, more important, causing needless problems and emotional turmoil for their employees. Almost without effort, the self-centered boss can sap employees' enthusiasm and smother their pride.

Some organizations use surveys or other instruments to measure the effect of leaders' personalities and management skills on their employees. These tools can affirm that a leader is a positive professional presence and are helpful in identifying someone whose egotism negatively impacts the work environment. Similarly, executives can conduct a self-assessment of their leadership style to determine the manner in which it influences subordinates. These processes are sometimes awkward but can provide valuable, new information about a leader's effectiveness and produce novel ways to improve superior-subordinate relationships.

- Implement a multilevel review of your performance, and use the results to improve or reinforce your leadership skills and increase your self-confidence.
- Seeing yourself as others see you is an honest reminder that it's not all about you.

TWENTY-SEVEN

Grandstands Are for the Circus

Every few months, a case of national importance creates a flurry of investigative activity in every FBI office. In these particular cases, FBI Headquarters officials typically contact the heads of all of the offices and task them with searching all files and records for particular names or other specific information. Agents and analysts review the relevant materials and then submit their findings, along with copies of the original source documents, to a designated point of contact in Washington.

Regardless of the search method used, someone is responsible for seeing that all of the pertinent files are reviewed. These jobs often fall to one of the more junior supervisors to enable them to gain experience in handling major projects and to allow their superiors a chance to evaluate their management skills.

In response to a major congressional inquiry involving one of these unusual cases, Kathleen's SAC directed her to handle one of these extensive reviews. The case was so complicated and touched on so many different aspects of the law that she had to ask the other supervisors in the office to assist her in combing through the files. To make matters worse, at that time there was no way to search for the pertinent reports electronically. As usual, headquarters officials had also set a short deadline.

Kathleen's peers were helpful in getting the project done, although some took much longer than others to conduct their file reviews and analyses. Nonetheless, it appeared that the office would produce a thorough report of its findings and meet the deadline set by headquarters.

Two days before the completed work was to be submitted to FBI Head-quarters Kathleen contacted the three supervisors who hadn't finished their tasks. She reminded them that they needed to complete their reviews as soon as possible and quietly hoped that they wouldn't let her down. Later that day, she attended the SAC's monthly manager's meeting, where the boss discussed Bureau activities and matters of importance in the field office. Toward the end of the meeting, the SAC asked everyone to update the group on their squad's activities.

When it was Kathleen's turn to talk, she brought up the congressional review project. She told the SAC that she had contacted the few supervisors who had yet to complete their reviews and expected that all of the work would be finished in time to meet the deadline.

Thinking that she had properly informed him of the status of the project, she was surprised when he asked her which of her coworkers had not yet completed their work. Kathleen didn't think their names were important as no one had missed a deadline, and she surely did not want to embarrass any of her peers. Knowing that she had to say something, however, she told her boss that she could not tell him who was lagging behind because she hadn't brought the list of names with her to the meeting.

The SAC was clearly not happy with her response.

"Are you saying you are not going to tell me who they are?" he said, his voice rising and his expression grim.

Kathleen shrugged her shoulders and naively looked around the table for someone who might help her out of this situation. The silence was broken, not by a helpful coworker, but by the boss's next unforgettable comment.

"You're grandstanding. Don't ever do that again, especially not at these meetings!"

Kathleen had not intended to "grandstand"; she hadn't withheld her co-workers' names in order to impress her peers with her discretion. Nonetheless, she instantly recognized the fragility of the superior-subordinate relationship and wished she had not brought up the matter.

Later that same day, Kathleen went to meet with the SAC in hopes of clarifying the intent of her remarks. At the end of their discussion, it was clear to him that he had interpreted her words in a way that was entirely different than what she had intended. As important, she also understood why he erroneously perceived her words as grandstanding. From this uneasy conversation came additional talks, and a professional friendship was generated as a result of these two awkward attempts to lead.

- Even when there is no intent to grandstand, it is the perception of the crowd that matters.
- Avoid making unnecessary comments about a peer's performance that could be perceived as negative.
- Some situations go bad so quickly that there is no way to recover.
- Leaders will likely remember their mistakes long after others have forgotten them.

TWENTY-EIGHT

Living Beyond Your Shadow

Most of us have known leaders with exceptional talents, men and women who seem to have it all—a brilliant mind, the ability to mesmerize an audience with their words and humor, and a natural commanding presence. Leaders with these positive qualities are a genuine asset to their organizations but only if they can live within the confines of their shadows.

Subordinates tend to admire these multitalented leaders although even well-deserved admiration can overcharge the leader's ego and cause him to live beyond his shadow as "Harry" did. His peers clearly saw that he was an intelligent, charming man with excellent leadership skills. Harry often consciously led others to believe that he was much smarter than they were, and in most instances he was. Notwithstanding his intellect and the respect of his employees, sooner or later he was certain to challenge the wrong opponent and create some serious problems for himself.

Many of Harry's subordinates were in awe of his willingness and propensity to confront others. Sometimes his employees would prod him to cross the line between aggressive and obnoxious behavior. Although Harry's opinions and conclusions were usually correct, he occasionally expressed them in a manner that demeaned his opponents. This type of unprofessional behavior is not acceptable in the FBI but was generally overlooked in light of Harry's stellar management capabilities and operational successes.

No one who knew Harry was surprised that he rose quickly in the FBI's ranks and was eventually named to head one of the Bureau's larger offices. The agents were happy to have a new boss of Harry's reputation and talents to direct them in the investigation of their many high-profile cases and to represent them to the public and in the law enforcement community.

In his new position, Harry regularly dealt with the leaders of other law enforcement agencies and enjoyed their respect—to a point. During a critical investigation being jointly developed by the FBI and other federal agencies, Harry and one of the agency heads had a serious disagreement about its direction. The other man was as strong willed as Harry was, and the agents fully expected that the issues would not be solved quickly or quietly.

Rather than keeping their differences of opinion private and contained, Harry made the mistake of trying to perform beyond his shadow. In an attempt to convert others to his point of view, he openly discussed the conflict with other law enforcement leaders and the agents involved in the investigation. Unfortunately, Harry's nemesis had considerably more political capital than Harry did, and when he learned of Harry's campaign to malign him, he took action of his own. He voiced his displeasure to his bosses in Washington and waited for the proverbial ax to fall on Harry.

When Harry's superiors at FBI Headquarters learned of his failure to keep his issues private and of the subsequent embarrassment this dustup had caused for the Bureau in the community, they were understandably angry. While most of them agreed that Harry's perspective on the original issue was correct, the manner in which he chose to address the problem was abhorrent. After receiving stern warnings by their respective agency heads, Harry and his adversary were told to resolve the matter locally, in a dignified and business-like manner.

These two formidable leaders half-heartedly attempted to settle their differences but to no avail. As their animosity toward one another grew, it became less likely that they would find a positive resolution to their conflicts. Nonetheless, Harry still secretly hoped to win the battle and made yet another attempt to garner external support by bringing the matter to the public's attention through the news media. Reporters were eager to pick up a story that pitted one federal agency against another—a tale made even more colorful by the egocentric personalities of the two key players. The resulting series of news stories chronicled a fascinating self-inflicted career wound that Harry should have seen coming.

The results of Harry's actions were extreme and completely predictable. By going to the press, he lost his battle, the admiration of many of his peers, and, most of all, the confidence of his bosses at FBI Headquarters. His discomfited superiors removed him from his position as a field commander and transferred him to Washington, D.C. His opponent, who was not removed from his job, won the fight and openly boasted about his role in having Harry removed from his prestigious assignment.

Harry's career tragedy and the embarrassment it caused his office and the FBI were unnecessary and the direct result of his propensity to live beyond his shadow. Years later, still living beyond that shadow, Harry tried to convince his peers that he had been treated unfairly by vitriolic detractors. As smart and capable as he was, Harry still had not learned that he was part of an organization and a culture that could not afford to tolerate his exaggerated sense of self.

- Dealing with conflicts privately prevents others, such as the media or detractors, from finding your Achilles' heel.
- Recognize and use power for what it is—namely, the temporary ability to control and influence others.
- Avoid absorbing power in such a way that it becomes indistinguishable from your character.

PART V

WHAT REALLY COUNTS

Many men and women desire to hold the top title in the office or on the battlefield for a variety of reasons. Some thrive on the institutional privileges that go along with being in charge. Others seek superior compensation and social status. There also are many, like the FBI's directors, who rightly believe that leadership is an opportunity to serve others and to share the lessons they have learned with those who follow.

Being the boss isn't right for everyone nor is it right for anyone all of the time. Every organization has its share of "accidental leaders," or those who find themselves in positions of authority and responsibility and later realize that the role is a perfect fit for their talents and personality. Other leaders—accidental or not—may discover after the fact that they are uncomfortable with the abstract division between the leader and his or her subordinates and should divest themselves of the mantle of authority. Similarly, men and women who require constant praise and those who find it difficult to extol the performance of others should reconsider their suitability to lead.

All of us are leaders and followers at different times and in different places. A well-cultivated organizational culture provides the proper environment for all of its members to flourish. What really counts is the knowledge of when you should lead and why.

TWENTY-NINE

The Accidental Leader

Occasionally men and women in the business world, government agencies, and nonprofit organizations are unexpectedly promoted to positions of responsibility. When an executive abruptly leaves a company or a leader becomes ill, even the most viable succession plan cannot prevent a hesitant employee from "accidentally" becoming the boss. New management positions frequently emerge from reorganizations or mergers that result in a corporate "battlefield promotion" of an unprepared staff member. Often, the most productive worker in the group will be designated as the boss with little regard for his or her leadership abilities.

Accidental leaders can become valuable assets to their companies if employees are properly prepared for the possibility. Top-notch future leaders can be developed through a robust mentoring program and by frequently receiving realistic leadership training. Individuals who have found themselves in unplanned positions of leadership have frequently benefited from the wisdom and guidance of their superiors, especially from those who took the time to show them how to be successful executives.

In the FBI, accidental leaders also strengthen their natural abilities through multilevel leadership training programs, reinforced by mandatory crisis management exercises. Although these strategies can be easily replicated in businesses and nongovernment organizations, they will not automatically turn a student into a leader. They will, however, help talented, diligent, and mission-oriented individuals improve their leadership skills and become vital assets to their employees and organization.

AN INAUSPICIOUS BEGINNING

Bill Gavin joined the FBI to fill the traditional role of a special agent and to investigate crimes, identify the perpetrators, and send them to prison. Once he finished his initial training, Director J. Edgar Hoover assigned him first to Minneapolis and then to Philadelphia. In those cities Bill investigated different types of crimes and chased and captured fugitives to his heart's content

Five years later, the head of the FBI laboratory arranged for Bill, who had a master's degree in biology, to transfer to FBI Headquarters. Despite the laboratory's worldwide reputation as a leader in forensic examinations, this move was not one Bill cared to make. Because there was no appeal process, Bill moved to Washington and made the best out of the unwanted assignment.

For the next five years Bill examined evidence submitted by law enforcement agencies throughout the country and conducted the required serology exams. He testified hundreds of times as to his scientific conclusions on murder, assault, and rape cases. All the while, however, he longed to return to the field and investigate cases of his own.

When Bill presented his case for a transfer back to the field to the assistant director (AD) responsible for laboratory operations, the AD urged him to stay in Washington. However, Bill was adamant about his desire to return to the field and even offered to transfer to any field office that might need him. After several minutes of discussion about Bill's personal goals and the needs of the FBI, the AD finally asked, "Have you ever considered going into management, Bill?"

Bill hadn't anticipated that question and quickly tried to gather his thoughts and explain why he didn't want any role in the management of the FBI.

The boss drew his line in the sand. "Look, Bill, becoming a manager is your only alternative. If you don't step up, then I can guarantee that you will spend the next twenty years in the lab. Besides that, you're always stirring up the other examiners. They listen to you and respect what you have to say. You'll be a good boss."

Bill saw that in order to return to the fieldwork that he loved, he had no choice but to take on a role of greater responsibility. He did as his boss suggested and volunteered to become a manager, which allowed to him to return to a field position. Although for a few years after their discussion Bill believed that his boss had failed him by not allowing him to return to the field as an investigator, he eventually came to realize that the AD's push to promote him to management had been a blessing in disguise. He committed himself to becoming a valuable manager. This accidental leader later experienced the euphoria of service when he was able to help an employee facing the personal demons of alcohol, to build partnerships with other law enforcement executives, to deal with an unprecedented crisis, and to be an understanding friend to a peer.

Bill tried to emulate those leaders for whom he had worked and whose reputations were enhanced by their passion for the job and their compassion for people. Every day he learned new things about management that made each subsequent assignment easier and more rewarding. Like so many other accidental leaders, Bill often found his unexpected leadership journey to be challenging, exciting, and deeply gratifying.

- The accidental *manager* is the individual who, lacking the enthusiasm to supervise others or to manage programs or projects, is appointed or promoted to a position of responsibility and muddles through.
- The accidental *executive* is the individual who, lacking the enthusiasm to supervise others or to manage programs or projects, is appointed or promoted to a position of responsibility and develops effective management skills.
- The accidental *leader* is the individual who is unexpectedly appointed or promoted to a position of responsibility and uses, and improves upon, his or her natural leadership qualities for the betterment of his or her colleagues and organization.

THIRTY

What Happened to All My Friends?

Not long ago "Larry," a longtime friend who was the SAC of a busy FBI office, called Bill Gavin and asked if Bill could stop by and see him the next time he was in town. Larry had spent more than thirty years investigating or directing some of the FBI's most complex cases and dangerous operations, and his recent promotion to one of the Bureau's most sought-after leadership positions was well deserved.

When Bill arrived at Larry's office, he could tell that he was anxious to go somewhere less hectic so that they could talk. As they left the building, Bill couldn't help but notice that Larry's demeanor was more subdued than in the past and his body language made Bill think he was carrying the weight of the world on his shoulders. Bill didn't have to wait long to find out what was bothering Larry.

"I hate my job, Bill," Larry said. "I should have stayed in the job I loved most—investigating cases, being part of the squad."

Bill was stunned by this revelation and Larry's feelings about being the boss. Bill had loved being the head of the FBI's offices in Miami, Denver, and New York and enjoyed having the ability to support the men and women who were catching criminals. He vicariously shared in their successes as they solved cases, gathered evidence that helped convict wrongdoers, and obtained restitution and justice for victims. He especially liked talking with the employees, getting to know them, and sharing in their lives. Being the boss allows you to do all that and more.

Larry tried to explain his problem to Bill, and maybe to himself. "My friends aren't my friends anymore. I don't think they trust me because I am the boss. We don't talk, we don't have drinks together—nothing. I am not sure who likes me and who doesn't."

Bill knew from other friends in the FBI that Larry was doing an exceptional job of running his office. Important investigations were under way, relationships with other law enforcement agencies were very smooth, and the executives at FBI Headquarters had a high regard for Larry's leadership style. His reputation among the troops was solid as well; he had been one of them for many years and the experience he brought to his new position gave him enormous credibility. The agents appreciated his low-key leadership style and how he would go to bat for them with FBI Headquarters when necessary.

Bill suspected that Larry's closest friends in the office might feel awkward about maintaining the same type of relationship they had with Larry before he became the boss because Larry appeared to be unsure of where to draw the line between leadership and friendship. Larry treasured the camaraderie he had shared with the other agents above all else, but he had been unable to effectively make the transition from peer to superior and still retain the personal bonds that he badly needed. Maybe he lacked the deep desire to lead or maybe he never understood the social risks of leadership. Regardless, Bill wasn't sure that he could do any more than to tell Larry to go back to the office and walk around.

"Sit with a couple of squads this afternoon," Bill recommended. "Ask the agents questions about their cases, their kids, their cars—anything. Start reconnecting. Let them know you like working for them and that your responsibilities have changed but you haven't."

Larry agreed to try to regain some of the closeness he had once had with his friends but he wasn't optimistic. He made some attempts to reconnect with his friends, but never became comfortable with the superior-subordinate relationship. A few months later, Larry called Bill to tell him that he was retiring and taking a job where he no longer had to be the boss.

As people have varying degrees of ability to lead, they also have different attitudes about being the leader. In most organizations—and the FBI is no exception—leaders enjoy greater status than non-leaders. Fortunately some very talented agents seek formal leadership roles, but that type of leadership responsibility requires personal adjustments that others would rather not make.

IF THE JOY DISAPPEARS

After Executive Assistant Director John Otto retired from the FBI, Kathleen McChesney, as the manager of the FBI's Executive Development and Selection Program, was assigned to report to Deputy Director Floyd Clarke. Every few weeks Kathleen would meet with Floyd to discuss vacant senior executive positions and to create a list of candidates to be considered for promotions or transfers. There were fewer than two hundred senior executives in the FBI at the time.

The position of deputy assistant director (DAD) in the Office of Professional Responsibility (OPR) became available when a long-term incumbent retired. Although this was an important, high-level position, it was not a pleasant job. FBI agents assigned to the OPR conducted all of the FBI's internal investigations, proving or disproving that an employee had violated a policy, acted improperly, or, in rare instances, had committed a crime. Though the work was a very crucial part of the FBI's administration, it was also far removed from the more exciting daily operations of investigating cases and prosecuting criminals.

Kathleen put together a list of names of likely candidates for the DAD-OPR position that included some SACs of FBI field offices and presented the list to Floyd. Floyd had other assignments in mind for a few of the candidates on the list but seemed interested in one person she had added at the last minute, David Binney. For the past year Dave had served as the SAC of the St. Louis office and was particularly well suited for the DAD position. A West Point graduate and Vietnam veteran with a wealth of management experience, Dave was the epitome of a leader and one of the most revered agents in the FBI. Although Floyd believed that SACs should serve a minimum of two years in their offices before being reassigned, he was more than willing to make an exception in Dave's case.

Ordinarily when Floyd identified a man or a woman he was considering for a promotion, he would thoughtfully call the agent to see if he or she had any personal or professional issues that would preclude a job change. On this day, however, Floyd was leaving town and asked Kathleen to call Dave on his behalf. Though it was somewhat unusual for her to call her superiors about their careers, she knew Dave and was looking forward to having a chance to talk with him.

Dave was surprised to get Kathleen's call and to hear of Floyd's interest in him for this position. He understood why Floyd hadn't called him personally, and, as was his modest nature, he was not offended that Floyd's subordinate had called him instead. Kathleen fully expected Dave to immediately ask her to convey his thanks for Floyd's confidence in his abilities and decline the offer.

To Kathleen's surprise, Dave became quietly reflective. As he spoke, she realized he was teaching her some important lessons about leadership and organizational culture.

"This is a shock, of course," Dave said. "I haven't been in St. Louis very long at all.

"I always wanted to be the SAC, you know. I had great hopes of being in charge of an FBI office one day, and I finally made it. The first few months were everything I expected it to be: working with dedicated people in a great office and a beautiful city, making close friendships in the law enforcement community . . . that sort of thing. Then it all changed when Doug was killed, and it has never been the same since."

Doug was L. Douglas Abram, an experienced FBI agent and member of the St. Louis SWAT team. In January of that year, Doug and his fellow team members were executing a search warrant at a house when one of the suspects shot Doug. Tragically, Doug died two hours later, the first agent from the St. Louis office to be killed in the line of duty.

Dave had suffered a loss so deep that he wasn't certain he could overcome it. Though Doug's death wasn't his fault, Dave felt responsible and even wondered if his employees might be better able to deal with Doug's death if he were to leave.

"You have to understand, Kathleen," Dave said. "I used to love this job. I love the people here, and I am their leader. But this shooting has changed my feelings. I have lost a family member. There is no joy here right now."

Kathleen wondered what to say to Dave. Clearly this kind and thoughtful leader was still struggling with what had occurred. Finally she said, "I'm sorry,

Dave. It's hard for anyone not in your shoes to understand what you're feeling or the pain Doug's family and his FBI friends are experiencing. What would you like me to tell Floyd?"

"Tell him I'll talk to my family."

Dave ultimately accepted the promotion and returned to headquarters a few months later as the deputy assistant director of the FBI's Office of Professional Responsibility. After Floyd Clarke retired, Director Freeh once again recognized Dave's leadership skills and selected him to take Floyd's place as the FBI's deputy director.

One afternoon as Dave was moving into the deputy director's office suite with its view of Pennsylvania Avenue and the Capitol, Kathleen stopped by to congratulate him. As he was showing her some of the law enforcement memorabilia he had collected during two decades of FBI service, he reminisced about their telephone conversation, which had led to the significant changes that had occurred in his life since then. He thanked her for calling him but was especially grateful that she had taken the time to listen to what he wanted to say about Doug Abram.

"I hope no FBI agent is ever killed in the line of duty again," he said. "But that's the risk of our business. One day, when you are in charge of your own office, you'll know that being the leader of an FBI office is the best job in the world—but sometimes it is the worst."

- Not everyone is cut out for a defined leadership role. If being part of the team is more fulfilling than leading the team, stay with the pack.
- Know when and how to draw the line between superior and subordinate, especially with those who are friends.
- It is important and healthy for the leader to maintain friendships with former peers.
- Occasionally circumstances will alter a leader's outlook and diminish his or her eagerness to lead.
- The realistic leader recognizes when he or she no longer has the desire to lead and steps aside for another leader to take his or her place.

THIRTY-ONE

Saying Thanks

Employees of all ranks are easily motivated by the gratitude of their leaders. The FBI has a system of rewarding employees for superior work, but the informal awards and demonstrated signs of appreciation are often equally as important. Sometimes the simple act of commending an employee publicly or calling or sending a personal note or e-mail message can be motivational and inspiring.

For nearly eighteen months, a squad of FBI agents in a midwestern city had been devoted to the investigation of a prominent la Cosa Nostra (LCN) family. The agents and their supervisor went through the challenging process of gathering evidence to establish probable cause and obtain authority from a federal judge to listen to and record the telephone conversations of the members of this organized crime group.

Before the investigation began, the agents had gained the approval of both the local U.S. attorney and of "Mike," the SAC of their office. They then conducted the tedious and time-consuming work of directing their informants to collect inside information from the suspects in the case, of debriefing the informants after their undercover meetings, and, of course, of verifying what the informants reported.

As in most organized crime cases, the agents conducted many hours of late-night surveillance because the crime family members, called wise guys by the agents, often conducted their business after dark. The agents also analyzed and reanalyzed their observations, attended dozens of conferences with FBI managers and federal prosecutors, and worked tirelessly at developing and implementing effective evidence-gathering strategies.

Their long hours and investigative efforts were at last rewarded when the agents obtained the legal authority to monitor the conversations of this LCN family. Ironically, this "reward" resulted in many more months of sixteen-hour workdays for everyone. Half of the squad was assigned to listen to the wise guys' calls, and the other half was assigned to follow leads, handle informants, and conduct surveillances. In other words, the agents' compensation for their perseverance on this case was additional hard work.

As usual, the agents on the squad continued to answer the bell each day, energized by overhearing LCN members actually planning or admitting to thefts, robberies, and other criminal acts. Translators and typists were called in to clarify and transcribe recorded conversations so that agents could follow new leads and provide regular reports to the court about the outcome of the wiretaps. The squad supervisor did double duty: in addition to keeping the workforce motivated and focused, he reviewed everyone's work to ensure the strict adherence to the numerous and complex administrative and legal requirements of a federal wiretap.

After sufficient information had been gathered to prove that these organized crime figures had planned or committed specific crimes, the phone lines were shut down. Through their work the agents had disrupted several criminal plots and built solid cases against many LCN family members and their associates. After the agents provided testimony to a federal grand jury, their targets were indicted for a variety of federal felonies. Their final step was to develop an extensive arrest plan and obtain and execute search warrants for the LCN members' hangouts and houses.

Following a grueling day of arresting their bad guys and collecting evidence, the weary agents gathered in their squad room to complete their paperwork, tie up loose ends, and congratulate one another. Mike stopped by at about 8 p.m. The agents took a break from their backslapping to listen to what their leader had to say about their case.

Those who expected affirmation, praise, or gratitude were immediately disappointed. Instead of gracious words in recognition of their achievements, Mike's first words were, "What's the next case in the pipeline?"

The agents began to glance quizzically at one another. A few thought their leader was kidding until he went on to direct everyone to get busy and concentrate on what needed to be done to develop the "next big investigation." After he finished his remarks, and being apparently not interested in any dialogue, this seemingly obtuse fellow headed for the door.

Once he was out of earshot, the squad supervisor waded into this regrettable set of circumstances. He tried to justify the boss's management style and approach by suggesting that the man was not prone to handing out compliments, even though he was impressed by what the squad had done. This hardworking group of men and women heatedly voiced their displeasure with their boss's attitude toward them. A few silently wondered why they had bothered to make so many personal sacrifices for this case.

As it happened in this case, Mike did not withhold praise because he wanted the spotlight for himself; in fact, he routinely shunned personal accolades. Rather, his intense, narrow focus on the FBI's mission prevented him from realizing the importance of thanking the employees who had done so much for their community and the Bureau. Sadly, Mike's chance to affirm the loyalty and commitment of his subordinates had passed, leaving them with a miserable impression of his leadership skills. While the agents continued to work just as diligently as before, few forgot this critical flaw in their leader's personality and the deflated feelings that followed.

IT'S FIVE O'CLOCK

A relatively small number of FBI agents in Detroit, and those assigned to its eleven satellite offices, are responsible for the investigation of federal crimes that occur throughout the large state of Michigan. When a particular case demands a substantial effort, all personnel must take part, despite their regular duties. Whining about performing a task that is not found in one's job description is not tolerated.

During his first week as SAC of the Detroit office, Hal Helterhoff met with his key contacts in the community, his law enforcement counterparts, and nearly everyone in the main office. By the end of the second week, he had visited with all of the employees in the satellite offices, traversing the state from Ann Arbor to Marquette and beyond. But it was by the end of the third week that he made his most significant impression on the office.

Hal understood the particular challenges of handling large or fast-breaking cases when personnel resources were as limited as they were in Michigan. He knew that regardless of the investigative skill of the individual FBI agent responsible for a challenging case, he or she would likely need some type of assistance from others. Hal also reinforced with his management team the importance of mutual assistance and of the need to convey that philosophy to their subordinates.

Soon after his arrival in Detroit, Hal was able to closely observe the employees' dedication to the mission and the organization in two fast-breaking violent crime cases. He saw these men and women arrive early and stay late, forgo meals, and, more important, miss irreplaceable time with their families and friends in order to get the job done. At 4 p.m. on Friday of his third week in Detroit, Hal picked up the phone on his desk and switched it to the public address mode. Those in the office were surprised when the SAC's voice came over the loudspeakers. "This is Hal. It's five o'clock. Have a good weekend and . . . thanks."

More than a few people in the office thought this message was a joke. Perhaps the boss was out and someone was imitating him, encouraging people to leave an hour early without authorization. Because nothing like this had ever happened before, a few employees contacted the one person who always knew what was going on in the office, Hal's secretary, Patty Waslyk. Patty knew that Hal wanted to recognize the extra time and effort spent by employees during the past few weeks and that he truly intended to let them leave early. As her phone started ringing and a few friends dropped by her office, Patty explained that Hal intended to express his gratitude to everyone in this new way.

Letting employees go home early now and then rarely merits a second thought in the private sector. However, a gesture of this sort is virtually unheard of in government offices, where bureaucratic rules often defy common sense and consideration. Hal knew that the Detroit employees deserved some recognition and, at minimum, a sixty-minute respite after generously pitching in to help one another on the important cases of the past few weeks. For the remainder of Hal's tenure in Detroit, the employees worked as hard as they ever did, but they also looked forward to those unexpected Friday nights when their boss would make a five o'clock announcement just to say thanks.

One of a leader's most important responsibilities is to develop and sustain a workplace environment where every employee knows that he or she provides value to the organization. This is easily done by recognizing your employees' personal sacrifices and results, as Hal did. But the leader must also remain alert for signs that subordinate managers may be disparaging or ungrateful to their direct team members. Where those behaviors are discovered, it is up to you to make certain they are corrected before they are imprinted on younger or newer coworkers who might make similar mistakes.

The importance of conveying gratitude to your employees cannot be overstated. In Mike's case, he failed as a leader when he squandered the opportunity to acknowledge a squad's exhaustive efforts and subsequent success on a major investigation. Although the agents continued to work as they had before, a few became unhappy and dispirited. Hal's employees, meanwhile, knew they were appreciated and became more enthusiastic and self-confident about their work.

- Leaders and subordinates occasionally disagree on the amount of effort each has expended on a task or the significance of the result.
- Learn when and how to thank your employees for their contributions.
- Be appropriately generous with your gratitude in order to inspire your employees and make your organization a better place to work.

THIRTY-TWO

Not Everyone Is Going to Like You

William (Bill) T. Rice Jr. was a brilliant, fun-loving supervisor in the FBI's Philadelphia office when he took a voluntary demotion to transfer to the Bureau's San Francisco office. Kathleen McChesney and Bill worked together on the organized crime squad there for a short time before the head of the office, SAC Robert Gast, realized that Bill was a talented leader who could add immediate value and experience to his management team. Mr. Gast reinstated Bill as a first-level supervisor and transferred him to the Oakland satellite office, and Kathleen was assigned there a few months later.

Had he not become an FBI agent, Bill would have made the perfect athletic coach. His physical stature, personal bearing, and deep voice created an imposing presence, and when he spoke everyone stopped to listen. Bill was also the ideal mentor. He enjoyed identifying talented men and women he believed would be good FBI leaders and encouraged them to volunteer for management positions through the FBI's career development program. Unlike the practices in some other organizations, FBI management positions are filled solely by volunteers who must compete for specific assignments in order to be promoted.

One early summer day, Bill had a serious discussion about leadership with Kathleen, and he encouraged her to write a memo to SAC Gast expressing her interest in becoming an FBI manager. Although Kathleen had eleven years of law enforcement experience, she had only been in the FBI for four of them and believed she had a lot more to learn about the organization if she wanted to consider managing others. She firmly declined to submit the paperwork, and that appeared to be the end of the discussion.

A few days later, Bill asked to see Kathleen about her request to take some days off for a vacation. He asked her if she had reconsidered entering the management program. Kathleen told him that she still wasn't interested. He grinned. "When you finally decide to apply, I will approve your vacation!" he said. "Until then, maybe you should just stick around."

Knowing that Bill was joking, Kathleen finally began to think seriously about his confidence in her abilities and his admonition that "sooner is better" if one hoped to learn as much as possible about leading others. After her vacation, Kathleen did as Bill suggested and signed up to become a manager. Thus began a series of training and mentoring sessions between Kathleen and some of the seasoned supervisors in the office, including Bill.

Besides teaching Kathleen about the FBI's administrative rules and operational procedures, Bill also shared some of his leadership philosophies, especially his belief that a leader's primary responsibility is to serve his or her subordinates. "Leading means guiding the team in ways that allows them to gain experience while building their confidence," he said. "It also means making sure you provide the agents with the resources and backing they need to do their jobs."

Bill also talked about the intrinsic rewards of being a leader. "Hey," he laughed, "you're not going to get rich doing this. I've moved my family half a dozen times across this country for Bureau promotions, and it's cost me money every time."

Though there were congressional proposals under way at the time to ease the financial burdens on federal agents who were transferred from one city to another, Kathleen had heard many horror stories about lost equity and unexpected expenses that had brought newly relocated managers to the edge of bankruptcy. Bill pulled out the federal government's General Schedule of Pay for FBI agents and mid-level managers and showed her the small difference between the salaries of supervisors and their subordinates. He also pointed out that a manager's pay raises, called step increases, were acquired through longevity and were minimal compared to the salaries of entry- and mid-level managers in the private sector.

"You might be lucky enough to get an incentive award [a cash bonus]," he said, "but supervisors rarely get them. It's more important that the agent who conducts the investigation be recognized for his or her efforts than it is for the boss to be honored. Don't ever forget to reward those people who have done a good job, or you'll sap their enthusiasm."

By then Bill knew that he hadn't painted a very rosy picture of being an FBI supervisor. There were long hours, additional responsibilities, and few incentives. Was there anything good about being an FBI manager?

"You're wondering why I do this, aren't you?" he asked. "It's many things, really. It's about knowing what's going on in the Bureau, the excitement of being a part of everyone's cases and of seeing your agents develop because you've been able to teach them something about making cases or conducting arrests. Being the boss is a lot of hard work. Some of your buddies will avoid you if you become the boss; others just won't like you because you're in charge. You'll spend a lot of time worrying about your responsibilities and the safety of your team. But at the end of the day, making a contribution as a leader is worth all that you put into it."

"Thanks, Bill," Kathleen said. "Any more advice?"

"Yes," he finished. "Don't ever expect them to thank you. If you hear those words, that's great, but don't count on it or judge yourself by how often your employees tell you they appreciate you. Don't expect everyone to like you, either."

THE SAFETY NET

Every FBI office has one or two agents who live on the edge. In their eagerness to make great cases, they take risks that seem brilliant if successful and harebrained if they fail. "Ronnie" was one of these agents, intensely throwing himself into his work and creating unique undercover scenarios that sometimes enabled him to gain valuable evidence against his targets.

One day Ronnie came up with a new scheme to infiltrate an organized crime gang. Ronnie knew that his supervisor, "Evan," would probably not approve of the plan, so he purposely did not tell him what he intended to do. After making certain that the plan did not violate any FBI policies, Ronnie and his partner went ahead with it. Their attempt to get into the group was an utter failure, but, luckily for Ronnie, it did not interfere with a related investigation.

Ronnie was not so fortunate later when his partner inadvertently mentioned the debacle to their boss during a chance encounter in the coffee room. Evan—red faced, furious, and fed up with Ronnie—went to see his boss, "Fred." Evan was nearly at his wit's end with Ronnie's shenanigans, however well intentioned they might be, and demanded that Ronnie be removed from his squad.

Fred thought it was important to hear Ronnie's explanation before deciding what steps to take. He brought Ronnie into his office later that day and listened thoughtfully as Ronnie acknowledged that he had crossed a professional line and been insubordinate to his boss. Ronnie knew that he deserved to be disciplined but begged Fred not to transfer him from the squad and cases that he loved. Fred knew that while Ronnie was a serious risk taker, he was also a dedicated and successful investigator. Ronnie's zeal reminded Fred a little of his own intense eagerness to succeed when he was a new and inexperienced agent. Fred wanted to believe Ronnie when he said he would toe the line in the future.

Fred thought about Ronnie's situation for a few days and waited for Evan to cool down. Although Ronnie had embarrassed Evan and set a very poor example for his peers, he was a dedicated employee who had a talent for inspiring his squad mates and a real passion for investigations. Finally, after discussing the situation again, Fred and Evan agreed that Ronnie would receive a written reprimand but would be allowed to remain on the squad.

Later in the week, after apologizing to his supervisor, Ronnie went to see Fred to thank him for letting him stay on the squad. He repeated his promise to be more careful in his work and more loyal to his supervisor. Ronnie had learned the hard way that a safety net in the hands of understanding leaders can break a fall.

Men and women join the FBI for the noblest of reasons—the chance to serve their communities and their country. By doing what they can to fulfill their mission—often at personal risk—FBI agents regularly do great things. Once in the FBI, agents are generally astute and aware enough to realize that the gravity of their mission trumps their normal need for pats on the back or awards.

Even the hardest-hearted law enforcement professional is grateful for an expression of gratitude for a job well done. The FBI offers few formal rewards for its top-level leaders and even fewer for its first-line and mid-level managers. Nonetheless, it's the small, personal rewards and expressions of appreciation that are the most meaningful and make every sacrifice worthwhile. Despite an occasional warning to the contrary, it is possible for a leader to be thanked—and to be liked.

- Regardless of a leader's popularity or exceptional interpersonal skills, there will be subordinates who will not like him or her merely because he or she is the boss.
- Before volunteering for a leadership role, you should believe that the contributions that you will make to the team and the organization outweigh the importance of being universally liked.
- As you transition from team member to team leader, anticipate changes in the group dynamic and take control of the changes to further a positive work atmosphere.

THIRTY-THREE

The Culture Club

Culture is more than simply the character of the organization; it is a dynamic reality sustained or sullied by its members. An organization's leaders are its cultural caretakers and are responsible for how the culture creates a family from strangers and leads it to success.

John Otto, the FBI's executive assistant director for Law Enforcement Services, impressed many people with his knowledge of the FBI, his grasp of the dozens of significant issues FBI leaders deal with each day, and the way in which he humbly and deftly performed his duties as the Bureau's acting director. Though some of his closest associates observed that John could be very passionate, even angry, when agents failed to do their best, most saw only his quick mind and attention to the task at hand.

Four of the FBI's six acting directors—John, Floyd Clarke, Thomas Pickard, and James B. Adams—came directly from the ranks of the Bureau. For FBI employees, having a director who understands and is a part of the FBI culture is reassuring. There is a deep bond of mutual respect between the employees and these in-house leaders that has been developed through shared experiences, perspectives, training, and commitment.

Being a part of the FBI, each of these acting directors had the advantage of having both macro and micro views of the organization. Their intricate understanding of both how and why thousands of FBI employees dedicate themselves to the Bureau's mission each day made it easy for them to be highly effective in their special roles. Each of these men "got it" in terms of understanding what drives the employees of this unique institution and in knowing how to influence the employees' professional behavior through their own example. Although their leadership styles and personalities were very different, they all were aware of what needed to be done, every day, to provide direction, resources, and encouragement to an already highly motivated workforce.

Shortly before John retired from the FBI, one of his employees stopped in his office to tell him that she would be having some surgery and be away from work for several weeks. Although she wasn't seriously ill, John was thoughtfully concerned.

At the time John was second in command of the FBI and had little opportunity for casual conversation. Nonetheless, he took the time then to discuss with her the importance of staying fit—John was an avid runner—and the value of good health.

To the woman's surprise, when she turned to leave John called out after her, "By the way, what's your blood type?"

"A positive," she replied.

"Me, too," he said. "I'll go down to Georgetown Hospital this afternoon and donate some blood for you."

This woman was overwhelmed when this busy executive offered to interrupt his important schedule to donate blood for her in the unlikely event that she would need a transfusion. Another FBI employee, Bill Imfeld, had already donated blood on her behalf and others were standing by if needed. It was deeply comforting to her to know that she had such good friends in the FBI.

Nearly speechless, the young FBI agent could only say, "Thank, you, Mr. Otto, but you don't have to do that."

His response was unforgettable and a clear reflection of the FBI's culture. "You are part of the FBI family. It is my privilege to help you."

THE RIGHT TO CRITICIZE

The astute leader recognizes when an organization's culture is inhibiting its growth or success. A leader with the right interpersonal skills can promote a positive culture that will motivate personnel and enhance the organization's brand and reputation. Improving the culture without disturbing its essence, however, requires the leader to have credibility and some shared history with his or her employees.

For the first seventy-five years of the FBI's history, nearly all of the executive, and most of the mid-level, management positions were filled by special agents. The special agents investigated cases, arrested criminals, and testified in court and were assisted by the other FBI personnel who, among other things, typed the agents' reports, issued their paychecks, and fixed their official cars. Despite their varied skills and talents, the employees who were not agents were lumped together in one large occupational category called support personnel. The support personnel, most of whom were women, had lesser stature in the organization as exemplified by their lower pay grades and limited promotional opportunities.

In the early 1980s, the FBI's human resources' functions began to more closely resemble those in other government agencies and the private sector. There were still only two main categories of employees, but the support personnel were now called professional support personnel in an attempt to rightfully acknowledge their capabilities and contributions. An increasing number of management positions were being created and filled by on-board professional support employees. Occasionally, an individual from outside the FBI was hired to supervise a group of professional support employees or to direct a specific project, especially if he or she had a particular expertise that could not be found within the organization.

As they began to be promoted to higher-level management and executive positions, the stature of the professional support employees increased. While agents still filled the top jobs, and especially those in Bureau operations, the non-agents began to be recognized for their expertise in information technology, finance, engineering, and human resources by being elevated to some of the FBI's senior levels.

There is a clear distinction between the job of an FBI agent and the hundreds of other jobs in the FBI, but all of the Bureau's employees share a similar culture of service. Although some members of Congress, government critics, and even a few national law enforcement leaders enjoy condemning the FBI culture, it is that very culture that has drawn generations of men and women to its doors when more lucrative work was available. The FBI's culture reflects the way in which its employees embody the FBI's values and maintain the personal and professional standards that set it apart from other organizations.

Some years ago, one of the FBI's top officials became concerned about a growing perception that the FBI's administrative practices were outdated and dysfunctional. To address this perception, and to correct any underlying problems that might have created it, he decided to bring in "Paul," an outside expert, to evaluate the Bureau's organizational structure and personnel procedures. Rather than hiring the man as a consultant, however, the official thought it best to make him a permanent employee and appointed him to an executive position at FBI Headquarters.

This arrangement put Paul in an awkward position. In his new role, he would be bogged down with the day-to-day work of his office and have little free time to concentrate on system improvements. More problematic was the fact that Paul would now be making some of the same administrative decisions that he was also expected to evaluate. Unfortunately, even after other FBI officials tactfully pointed out to Paul's superior that there appeared to be a conflict of interest created by Paul's assignment, no changes were made.

At first Paul seemed pleased, and even proud, to become one of the few high-level executives in the FBI, but once on board he lost no time in openly criticizing the way the FBI conducted its business. Although some of the Bureau's administrative processes were laudable, many of its policies and procedures were, in fact, still broken or in need of improvement. The FBI was in the process of fixing these problems, and many employees had noticed that the Bureau was headed in a new direction. The employees were just beginning to gain more confidence in the FBI's policies and procedures when Paul arrived.

Instead of learning his primary job when he came on board, Paul focused his attention on a few specific administrative matters. He quickly—and inaccurately—determined that most of the FBI's administrative procedures were worthless. Although changes were under way to improve several systems, Paul would not acknowledge those efforts. To the consternation of his new coworkers, Paul also claimed that many of the FBI's problems were the result of its culture, which he mistakenly perceived as discriminatory.

When it looked as if Paul was headed for a major ruckus with his new coworkers, "Molly," one of the senior managers, arranged a meeting with him to figure out ways he could work more effectively with her and her team. Their conversation began with Paul reciting a litany of wide-ranging problems existing within the FBI. Paul was proud that he had managed to ferret out these problems in less than five days on the job.

Whether Paul's quick assessment of the Bureau's issues was even partly accurate, as a new employee (and a person of some authority) he should have realized that by immediately voicing his criticisms of the organization to a loyal career employee, it would be difficult for him to gain her backing for any of his future initiatives. Substantive problems that he may have hoped to resolve were overshadowed by the negative way in which he framed his message. Molly found their meeting disappointing and deeply frustrating.

Not long after his discussion with Molly, Paul reasserted that the FBI's culture had to change completely in order to solve its administrative difficulties. Paul may have believed his imprimatur to disparage the FBI's culture came by way of being handpicked by a top executive to help the FBI deal with important issues. Instead of focusing on positive or creative solutions and embracing and utilizing what was beneficial about the FBI culture, however, he chose to continually berate the organization. He believed the FBI's much needed transformation could occur based solely on his direction.

Paul continued to reiterate his list of FBI "wrongs" to other managers, to various employee groups, and even to executives from other government agencies. Although he was right in wondering if the FBI culture had any impact on its administrative procedures, he did not take the time to fully understand the culture before reaching that conclusion. As his peers expected, Paul's well-intentioned approach was notably unsuccessful.

People are attracted to careers in organizations that have a mission and a culture that mirrors their personal values. The organizational culture in particular enhances camaraderie and contributes to the employees' sense of belonging. As long as the mission and culture are stable and integrated, employees are more likely to be loyal and committed. Organizational cultures can collapse quickly, however, if leaders fail to recognize their importance or foolishly substitute organizational pride with arrogance. Fortunately, most FBI leaders understand the singular nature of the Bureau's culture and recognize their responsibility to nurture it for future generations of employees.

- Work for your organization rather than against it.
- Members of an organization, and especially its leaders, must earn the right to criticize.

- Refrain from criticism until you are sufficiently knowledgeable about an organization and can offer solutions to problems in a positive, constructive, and respectful way.
- Exercise organizational pride rather than arrogance.
- Appreciate the organizational culture and the important role the leader plays in sustaining it.

THIRTY-FOUR

Leaders of Leaders

"Leaders of leaders"—the individuals at the highest levels in an organization—have special responsibilities to their employees and to their constituents, be they stockholders, donors, or taxpayers. These men and women set the tone and direction of the organization and are the final arbiter of conflicts. Most important, as they represent their organization to the world, they have the ability to single-handedly enhance, or damage, its reputation or brand. It has been the FBI's good fortune to have had six permanent directors who were all true leaders of leaders. Each seemed to cherish his duties and, in his own unique style, made the right choices and changes that successively contributed to building a better and more dynamic FBI.

Every organization—whether a global conglomerate, an iconic charity, or a government agency, like the FBI—is measured in large part by the quality, character, and professionalism of its leaders. While the performance of all of the employees is extremely important to the way the organization is perceived, it is the leadership of the person at the top that sets the standard and sometimes tips the scales of public favor and acceptability. If the leader displays high ethical standards, the organization will benefit. But if the leader falls short of these expectations, the impact on the organization's image can be disastrous.

When contrasting the leadership of the FBI's six permanent directors, and its six acting directors, it is clear that all of them have demonstrated superior personal and professional integrity. Naturally, every director had a unique leadership style, yet each one brought credit to the institution and to the country in a special way. In examining the totality of their performances it is clear that despite the differences in their managerial styles, all of the directors lived up to the FBI's core values and had great and historic accomplishments during their tenure.

It is important to consider, too, that as the FBI's responsibilities have changed over time, so have its leadership needs. The fledgling institution of the 1920s likely required the more autocratic style of J. Edgar Hoover, whereas the internationally expanding organization of the 1990s needed the visionary approach of Louis Freeh. The FBI's six directors have taken the Bureau down different paths, but they always stayed focused on the same intrinsic goal of keeping the nation secure and protected.

J. EDGAR HOOVER (1936–1972)

J. Edgar Hoover, who died in 1972 while still in office, is the best known of all the FBI directors. Director Hoover headed the Bureau of Investigation, an arm of the U.S. Department of Justice, from 1924 until 1936. He agreed to take on the responsibility of the job only after Attorney General Homer Stille Cummings assured him that the Bureau would not become a catchall for political hacks as it had been in the past. Hoover was given the authority to hire and fire the staff as he saw fit, and he pledged to make all future appointments based on merit and all promotions based on proven ability. Furthermore, he insisted that he report only to the attorney general.

When he took over the Bureau of Investigation, it was a disjointed and dysfunctional organization comprised of criminal investigators who, for the most part, had obtained their positions through political patronage. Once Hoover was given broad administrative authorities by the attorney general, however, he was able to depoliticize the organization and greatly improve its public image. In 1936, when the Bureau of Investigation became a distinct federal agency and was renamed as the Federal Bureau of Investigation, Hoover became its first director.

The management model created under the conditions that existed in the new FBI provided substantial power to the new director. Reinforced by Hoover's non-collaborative style and his persona as an aloof leader, many of the employees perceived him as dictatorial. This seemingly absolute power often prevented Hoover from hearing opinions different from his own and, consequently, from exploring better alternatives of action. In retrospect, it seems certain that the leadership actions of the FBI would have been enhanced through a participatory management arrangement. Furthermore, had he embraced the concepts of cultural, racial, and gender diversity, it may have strengthened the FBI's reputation for impartiality and objectivity.

A popular tale about Hoover's style exemplifies how fearful his closest colleagues were of him, even hesitating to ask him simple questions. As the story goes, the director came into his office one morning and off-handedly inquired as to the "status of the borders." Perhaps this is more a testament to the weaknesses of his subordinates than to Hoover's ability to provide clear directions, but soon agents were dispatched from the FBI offices adjacent to Canada and Mexico to look for any signs of trouble and report back immediately to FBI Headquarters. While this example is an amusing anecdote, Hoover's management style discouraged his subordinates from asking clarifying questions or making recommendations for operational and administrative improvements.

It took some time for Director Hoover to achieve his initial objectives for the FBI, but he eventually created the framework of the efficient, effective law enforcement agency it is today. He used his ultimate authority over the FBI to mold it into a law enforcement organization that set the standard for others to follow. He had the foresight to establish the FBI laboratory and conduct forensic examinations for other federal and state law enforcement agencies and to create the FBI's Fingerprint Division as a national repository of criminal and civil fingerprint records.

With J. Edgar Hoover, there was never any doubt as to who was in charge. Like the leaders of most other organizations, he made decisions that did not always prove to be correct, but, despite his mistakes, he held his position for decades. To his credit, Director Hoover used the civic platform to gain financial and political backing for the Bureau, notwithstanding some of the other, less principled methods he is believed to have used to retain that support. Although his performance has been primarily measured by using the management standards of a later time, his extraordinary tenure was marked by many more successes than failures.

L. PATRICK GRAY (1972–1973)
When Hoover died in 1972, President Richard M. Nixon appointed L. Patrick Gray as the acting director of the FBI. Trying to step into the shoes of a

legend would be a difficult task for anyone—even for Gray, a proven military leader. His time as director was both brief and chaotic, brought on by a series of events in which Gray was a victim of some of the questionable acts of his colleagues and some poor decisions of his own.

As a graduate of the U.S. Naval Academy and a career naval officer, Gray was totally committed to following the mandates of his commander in chief. He was not prepared to act in a totally independent manner, to refuse a request he believed came from the president of the United States, or even to suggest an alternative course of action to his superiors. Responding to the power of the White House, he destroyed documents seized from the safe of E. Howard Hunt, the organizer of the Watergate break-in. To make matters worse, he provided information about the FBI investigation to the White House counsel—an act that sealed his fate and future with the FBI.

Gray's missteps unfortunately overshadowed the many actions he took to better the FBI in his year as acting director. Within days of taking over the helm of the FBI, he had authorized women to become special agents, which Director Hoover had believed would be harmful to the Bureau's image. This particular step was long overdue, and within weeks women were applying to become a part of a historic change in an institution whose culture had stagnated.

WILLIAM RUCKELSHAUS (1973)

In April 1973, President Nixon removed L. Patrick Gray from his position and replaced him with William Ruckelshaus. Ruckelshaus was a very talented lawyer who served only a few months before Clarence M. Kelley became the FBI's second permanent director. Ruckelshaus was then designated as the deputy attorney general and continued to have a positive influence on the FBI.

His leadership skills and his character were most evident in a notorious incident known as the Saturday Night Massacre. Ruckelshaus and his boss, Attorney General Elliot Richardson, publicly resigned their positions rather than obey an order from President Nixon. The president had directed the men to fire prosecutor Archibald Cox, who was investigating the Watergate break-in for which Nixon had serious culpability. As this political drama unfolded, it was clearly time for some stable leadership at the FBI.

CLARENCE M. KELLEY (1973–1978)

Clarence M. Kelley was the first of the subsequent permanent directors to be nominated for the position by the president of the United States and confirmed by the U.S. Senate. Kelley became an FBI agent in 1940 and rose through the ranks to become the SAC of the Memphis office. After he left the Bureau in 1961, this highly competent law enforcement leader was appointed to be the chief of police in Kansas City, Missouri.

From his previous decades of service in the Bureau, Kelley knew the responsibilities of being the FBI director and the personalities and capabilities of many of its officials. He fully understood the absolute necessity of implementing several long-overdue internal reforms. He was also acutely aware of the customs and ways of the organization that had prevented earlier changes and the internal challenges he might face in creating a better FBI.

To dispel some of the negative images of the Bureau and the public misperceptions of its secret operations, Director Kelley sought the assistance of the General Services Administration (GSA). In an unprecedented move, he invited GSA officials to travel with the FBI's internal inspectors to evaluate the effectiveness and efficiency of operations of the FBI field offices. By opening up the FBI's self-evaluation process to external scrutiny, Kelley also opened himself up to some internal criticism. The much-lauded success of this endeavor, however, turned the subtle disapproval into future endorsements for greater organizational transparency.

Director Kelley was a highly approachable leader who sought the diverse opinions of contemporaries and peers in order to avoid the formulation of policy in a vacuum. He was often described as a "breath of fresh air" for his openness and candor when making decisions. By contrast, Director Hoover was noted for his domineering style of leadership. From his experience as a police chief, Kelley knew well the importance of cooperation between federal and state agencies, and he fostered such relationships in a more amicable fashion than Hoover had.

Kelley's reputation as a family-oriented man of high values was reflected in the way he cared for the FBI's thousands of employees. Regardless of their position, he treated everyone equally and demanded that the other FBI leaders do the same. Director Kelley naturally identified with the workers "in the trenches," and he did all that he could to further their work and initiatives. For example, the establishment and institutional acceptance of undercover and sting operations occurred under Director Kelley's leadership. He also initiated the utilization of computers in the FBI as he had done for the police department in Kansas City.

Some who knew him described Director Kelley as being a little "rough around the edges," but all of them cherished his leadership abilities. Those abilities helped to leverage the FBI into a new era of crime fighting and gave the agents a greater understanding of the broader picture of law enforcement. His personal style caused employees to work harder, and he regularly promoted the concept that it was better to do your best and take a chance on "stubbing your toe" than to do the minimum in order to avoid possible criticism. When he announced his second retirement after five years at the helm of the FBI, many wondered if this exceptional, thoughtful leader could ever be replaced.

JAMES B. ADAMS (1978)

James B. Adams, a highly regarded FBI agent and executive, was named acting director of the FBI after Director Kelley's departure. He served for only eight days in early 1978 before Judge William H. Webster was sworn in as the FBI's third director.

WILLIAM H. WEBSTER (1978–1987)

The undercover operations that were inaugurated by Clarence Kelley were remarkable for their creativity and results. When Kelley left the Bureau in 1978, it fell to William Webster to continue to authorize these unique types of investigations. Few law enforcement officials, perhaps even a former federal judge like Webster, could have envisioned the historic successes or the innumerable legal issues of some of these cases.

Although the FBI has conducted many undercover operations, few have been as well known as the ABSCAM case of the late 1970s and early 1980s. When this investigation concluded, a U.S. senator, several congressmen, and state public officials were convicted of bribery and tax evasion, and the public and political interest in the FBI's techniques was high. The ability to conduct this investigation had required the courageous and unwavering commitment of the FBI director, from its inception to its subsequent congressional review.

Director Webster was keenly aware that ABSCAM, when revealed, could cause the FBI to lose some congressional advocates. Nonetheless, after reviewing all of the related legal issues, he followed the law and approved each aspect of the operation. His meticulous research and careful deliberations later proved to legislative reviewers that he had done everything possible to guarantee the constitutional protections of every potential defendant.

Like Director Clarence Kelley, William Webster was also an attorney, and he had spent most of his career in legal roles. By the time he was nominated by President Jimmy Carter to lead the FBI, Webster had been a U.S. attorney, a federal district court judge, and a member of the U.S. Court of Appeals for the Eighth Circuit. He was known to be a man of high intellect and fairness and a good fit for the organization, which was still being roundly criticized for the misjudgments of its first director.

Despite his knowledge of FBI investigations, Webster had a lesser understanding of the agency's bureaucracy. After Congress approved his appointment in 1978, he wisely took the time to learn the job and all that he could about the Bureau's culture and its people. He also recognized the importance of working with individual senators and representatives and cultivated relationships with them. As he gained their acceptance, he enhanced his personal credibility and that of the FBI.

Director Webster was intent on advancing the Bureau during the course of his stewardship, and he was equally committed to seeing that the steps of progress were made within the parameters of existing rules, regulations, and laws. He strongly informed the FBI's employees of the professional standards that he expected the men and women of the nation's largest and best-known federal law enforcement agency to meet.

Director Webster displayed a sharp intellect, foresight, and common sense during his term as director. When it came to making decisions, he listened to all of the facts and conclusions presented by his advisers. He was highly inquisitive and—to the chagrin of a few—often asked many additional questions before approving an action or selecting a new senior leader. To his credit, and to good result, he favored a participatory management style and valued the opinions of the FBI's executive team, which he had inherited when he became the director.

Leading by example was part of William Webster's management approach. This was especially evident in his contacts with Congress, and as a result of his character, ethical standards, and candor, he maintained their confidence for nearly a decade.

Although Director Webster was not "of the Bureau" in the same sense that Directors Hoover and Kelley had been, his nine years as its leader were marked by numerous successes. He was held in high esteem by his employees and public officials, and his ability to navigate the legal and political waters in Washington was much admired by President Ronald Reagan, who named him as the director of the Central Intelligence Agency (CIA) in 1987. As the only individual to have been the director of both prestigious agencies, Webster was able to integrate aspects of their work in new ways that brought long-lasting benefits to the nation's intelligence community.

JOHN E. OTTO (1987)

John E. Otto, the FBI's executive assistant director, stepped into the role of acting director when Director Webster moved on to the CIA. For the next six months, Otto ran the organization with great skill and dedication. Not one to take on the trappings of the office, Otto declined to have a driver, answered his own mail, and returned every phone call within a day. He was noted for his efficiency and not wasting time when decisions needed to be made. More important, Otto recognized the need for the Bureau's employees to maintain a healthy balance between work and family.

WILLIAM S. SESSIONS (1987–1993)

By the time the Senate confirmed William Sessions as the FBI's fourth director, the Bureau had more than twenty-four thousand employees. The transparency of FBI operations that had come about under the leadership of Directors Kelley and Webster now presented a tremendous challenge to the new director. Although the increased openness had raised congressional and public confidence in the agency, the additional media scrutiny was occasionally a distraction to the Bureau's leaders.

Director Sessions, like William Webster, had extensive legal experience as a litigator, federal district court judge, and U.S. attorney. At the time of his nomination to the FBI post in 1987, Sessions was the chief judge of the federal court in the Western District of Texas, where he had developed trusted relationships with many administrators and attorneys. Once he had secured the FBI appointment, Judge Sessions invited several of these men and women to come and work for him at the Bureau. All were bright, well-intentioned professionals, but not all of them were fully prepared to provide a new director with the kind and quality of counsel that he needed to succeed.

Director Sessions indicated to his executives that he would lead by delegating authority and building consensus. Unfortunately, much of the delegating and decision making was left to his inexperienced, imported staff rather than to the FBI leaders who would have provided him with the same quality of advice that they had given his predecessor.

During Director Sessions's tenure at the FBI, the organization had many investigative successes and improved the way in which personnel resources were managed. As director, Sessions championed the causes of minorities and women and saw to it that they were treated fairly in terms of their assignments, promotions, and disciplinary matters. He was strong in his belief that a diversified workforce at all levels would produce a better organization and insisted on receiving daily updates regarding hiring and promotions. In his speeches to Bureau employees, as well as in his public remarks, he often raised the issue of the need for equal employment opportunities in the FBI, and he encouraged full participation in leadership development. Despite the fact that progress was being made, however, the director was forced to deal with legal challenges from Hispanic and African American employees regarding their representation in management positions in the Bureau.

Several serious incidents occurred during Sessions's six years as FBI director that tested his leadership skills and those of his senior executives. The shooting of the wife of a fugitive in Ruby Ridge, Idaho, by an FBI sniper in 1992 and the conflagration that resulted in the loss of many lives during a raid on the Branch Davidian Compound in Waco, Texas, in 1993 generated significant criticism of the FBI and may have impacted Sessions's image as its leader. He firmly supported the internal and external reviews of these incidents, however, and implemented the changes to the FBI procedures and protocols that arose from them.

To make matters worse, in 1997, an FBI laboratory examiner made serious allegations as to the science, protocols, expertise, and testimony of some of the other examiners. The accusations prompted an investigation by the Department of Justices's Office of the Inspector General. Subsequently, the inspector general criticized some of the FBI's laboratory operations and mandated major changes in the way forensic science was applied to the analysis of evidence. While Director Sessions was not directly responsible for any of the scientific shortcomings, as the head of the organization he accepted responsibility for its failures.

Director Sessions was an enthusiastic successor to the role of FBI director and was kind to and engaging with all employees. Nonetheless, critical institutional problems, not of his making, continued throughout his term. The more serious issues, however, were the allegations made against him personally that involved the improper use of FBI equipment and funds. The director's boss, Attorney General Janet Reno, found he had shown serious deficiencies in judgment, and in July 1993, she dismissed him from his position.

FLOYD I. CLARKE (1993)

Director Sessions's departure was followed by the appointment of Deputy Director Floyd I. Clarke as acting director in July 1993. This was a difficult period for the FBI. Clarke maintained the high road, however, and refused to fall prey to media attempts to discredit his former boss. The consummate professional, he demonstrated very well that career FBI agents, like him, could effectively lead the FBI and deal with its crises as well as its critics.

LOUIS J. FREEH (1993–2001)

A leader who has had experience at some level in an organization has a distinct advantage over someone who does not. In that regard, as former FBI agents, Directors Clarence Kelley and Louis Freeh were able to become effective leaders in a rapid fashion. Both Kelley and Freeh were intimately familiar with FBI procedures, policies, and special customs that were important to employee morale. They also knew the capabilities of the employees and whom they could rely on for their guidance and leadership abilities.

Unlike Clarence Kelley, however, Louis Freeh had not spent many years in the FBI before becoming director. Kelley had held most of the FBI's key leadership positions and had the benefit of understanding the varied perspectives of superior and subordinate. Freeh, on the other hand, had not held executive-level positions in the Bureau prior to leaving to become an assistant U.S. attorney and, later, a federal court judge. In addition, when he was selected by President Bill Clinton to replace Director Sessions in 1993, Freeh was only forty-three years old, the youngest of the FBI's five directors.

Notwithstanding his age, Louie, as he preferred to be called, was a strong and assertive leader who expected employees to adhere to the organization's rigorous standards and values. His personal demonstration of steadfast ethical behavior and dedication to the Bureau and its employees were emulated by his subordinates. Anyone who failed to live up to these standards did not become part of Freeh's leadership cadre.

During his eight years as FBI director, several major investigations tested Freeh's strength and leadership ability, including the Olympic Centennial Park bombing, the bombing of the Murrah Federal Building in Oklahoma City, the explosion of TWA flight 800, and even the investigation of Robert Hanssen, FBI agent and Russian spy. Director Freeh is an extremely intelligent individual who is capable of rapidly grasping the essence of a discussion or identifying a solution to a problem; as a result he was well equipped to address the myriad issues associated with these cases. Each decision that he made, in these cases as well as in others, was for the good of the country and the Bureau and never for himself.

Of Louis Freeh's many leadership qualities, his vision was one of the most valuable to the FBI. When he became director, Freeh immediately recognized that the Bureau's investigative reach had exceeded the U.S. borders. Although there were federal laws directing the FBI to conduct extraterritorial investigations involving U.S. citizens, the Bureau wasn't fully organized, staffed, or trained to work internationally.

To become more familiar with the global environment and establish relationships with the heads of law enforcement agencies in other countries, Director Freeh traveled extensively. Once he saw the overwhelming demands placed on the FBI agents detailed to small FBI offices in two dozen countries, he spearheaded an expansion of the FBI's international program by personally contacting key members of Congress to solicit their assistance. Gradually Freeh succeeded in increasing the number of agents and translators assigned to overseas posts, enabling the FBI to provide a rapid response to major crimes involving American citizens abroad and to interact more closely with their foreign law enforcement counterparts.

During his frequent travels to the FBI field offices, Director Freeh encouraged agents and managers to be proactive in their duties but always operate within the confines of laws, rules, and regulations. Except when pressed for time, he used these visits to speak to all of the employees and to the leaders of local law enforcement agencies.

Director Freeh's devotion to the FBI was unparalleled and reflected in the way he led the organization and in his personal interaction with each worker. By managing to conduct himself according to the core values of the FBI (a list of which he always carried on a printed card in his suit jacket), he had many admirers and few detractors. Although he was occasionally criticized for his tendency to evaluate his executives primarily through the eyes of the field agents, the praise he received from FBI employees for that approach endures.

THOMAS J. PICKARD (2001)

Thomas J. Pickard, another career FBI agent like Floyd Clarke, was appointed as the acting director when Director Freeh left his position in June 2001. Also like Clarke, Pickard was second in command as the deputy director and familiar with every aspect of the organization. Tom had worked side by side with Director Freeh through some of the FBI's most difficult cases and challenges and was an extremely capable and well-liked leader throughout the transition between Director Freeh and Robert Mueller.

ROBERT S. MUELLER III (2001–PRESENT)

In identifying a replacement for Director Freeh, President George W. Bush looked to the legal community, as had Presidents Reagan and Clinton, rather than looking inside the FBI for a capable candidate. Robert S. Mueller III, the U.S. attorney from San Francisco, emerged as an early prospect and easily won confirmation by Congress.

Mueller, like his predecessors Kelley, Webster, Sessions, and Freeh, is an attorney with an extensive record of public service. When he became the FBI director in September 2001, he was able to quickly and effectively use the leadership skills that he had developed as a young Marine Corps officer, and then refined in management positions in the Department of Justice, to guide the Bureau through the investigation of the al Qaeda terrorist attacks in the United States.

Director Mueller's management style is collaborative in that he seeks the facts from, and opinions of, others—even in some situations where he may already know what his decision will be. Although some subordinates might be discouraged when their suggestions are not accepted, this approach can help them to become better leaders and decision makers by motivating them to be well prepared for their discussions with the director. Mueller's low-key yet aggressive personality lends itself well to dealing with the many changes and challenges the FBI has faced in recent years. He strives—as he expects other to strive—for continuous improvement in all aspects of the organization, be it implementing a cutting-edge technology or hiring a world-class expert to correct a problem.

Though his tenure as the FBI's sixth permanent director is likely to be described as transformational, Mueller is a strong protector of the key tenets of the FBI and its formidable place in the international security arena. He has had to balance the pressing need for improvements in the way in which American law enforcement agencies investigate and prevent acts of terrorism with the need to investigate some of the nation's most complex fraud and sensitive corruption cases. Maintaining this balance requires the continued advocacy of Congress and the executive branch, something that Director Mueller has cultivated with much success.

- An organization's leader often is the personification of its brand and reputation.
- An organization is often known more for the character of its leaders than for what it produces.
- The leader of leaders is expected to provide the organization's vision and the strategy to fulfill its mission.

THIRTY-FIVE

What It Takes

Being a leader is a process that begins with having the fundamental intelligence, interpersonal skills, and value system necessary to meet the inevitable challenges that come with responsibility. But being a leader requires more than the fundamentals; it takes time, courage, and determination as well. Great leaders avoid rushing to the top of the mountain; rather, they climb it carefully enough to learn where the tough spots are along the way and figure out how to overcome them.

Leaders have the courage to make decisions once they realize that they have sufficient knowledge to do so—knowledge derived from the combination of vital information and personal experience. They have no fear of engaging in a critical self-assessment of their abilities and performance and are rationally introspective about their desire to lead. They demonstrate, through their actions and words, that they are determined to be known not just as highly competent and visionary leaders, but also as leaders who pick up their own brass.

APPENDIX

Comparable FBI and Business Leadership Positions

FBI LEADERSHIP POSITIONS	BUSINESS LEADERSHIP POSITIONS
• FBI Director	• Chief Executive Officer/ President
• FBI Deputy Director	
	• Chief Operating Officer
• Assistant Director	• Executive Vice President
• Special Agent in Charge	
• Inspector	• Senior Vice President
• Section Chief	• Vice President
• Unit Chief	
	• Director
• Assistant Special Agent in Charge	
	• Manager
• Supervisor/Program Manager	
• Supervisory Special Agent	• Lead
• Special Agent	• Administrative Support
• Administrative Support (Non-Agent)	

The FBI's Executive Development and Selection System is a voluntary process. FBI special agents can choose to spend their entire careers as investigators, or through a series of competitive steps, they may move up through the ranks in both field operations and administrative positions in headquarters. Promotions to higher ranks in the FBI have both basic and specific requirements and often involve relocation. Nearly all progression is from one rank to the next higher level, although occasionally an individual will skip a level and be promoted to a higher position at the discretion of the FBI director.

Most U.S. based businesses and the military have a distinct pyramid-style leadership structure as does the FBI. In recent years a "flatter" leadership model has been adopted by a number of businesses to encourage greater collaboration and effectiveness. Such a system has not been adopted by the FBI.

ABOUT THE AUTHORS

KATHLEEN McCHESNEY, PhD

During her twenty-four-year career as a special agent of the Federal Bureau of Investigation, Kathleen McChesney rose through the ranks to become the first female special agent to reach the position of executive assistant director—the FBI's third highest position—where she was responsible for leading seven major FBI divisions. She had also headed the FBI's field offices in Chicago and Portland, Oregon, and held management positions in the Los Angeles, San Francisco, and Detroit field offices and at FBI Headquarters in Washington, D.C. Before joining the Bureau, Kathleen was a King County police officer and detective in Seattle and part of the homicide task force that investigated serial killer Ted Bundy.

In 2002 Kathleen was named the first executive director of the Office of Child and Youth Protection of the U.S. Catholic Bishops Conference. She established the church's national standards to prevent child abuse and worked with the John Jay College of Criminal Justice to conduct the only comprehensive research study of the incidence of sexual abuse of minors by Catholic clergy. Kathleen became vice president of Global Security for the Walt Disney Company in 2005 and is currently the CEO of Kinsale Management Consulting, a woman-owned firm that provides leadership advice to businesses and not-for-profit organizations.

Kathleen holds a BS in police science and administration from Washington State University, an MA in public administration from Seattle University, and a PhD in public administration from Golden Gate University. She has published numerous articles on law enforcement topics and has taught courses at Seattle University and the King County Police and FBI Training Academies. She has been honored with the U.S. President's Meritorious Achievement Award, the Lifetime Achievement Award for Women in Policing, an honorary PhD from Anna Maria College, and the Hildegard Van Bingen *Woman for the World* Award. Kathleen serves on several boards and lives in Los Angeles.

WILLIAM A. GAVIN

William A. Gavin began his twenty-seven-year FBI career as a special agent investigating criminal matters in Minneapolis and Philadelphia. He served in management roles at FBI Headquarters and in the St. Louis and Kansas City field offices and as the special agent in charge of the Denver field office. He was later appointed as the assistant director of the FBI's Inspection Division. In this critical position, Bill was responsible for assessing the efficiency, effectiveness, and economy of FBI operations throughout the country and its international locations. Bill also directed the work of the FBI's inspection teams that were responsible for investigating the agency's most sensitive internal affairs cases and for providing long-range planning for the Bureau.

Bill later headed the FBI's Miami field office as the special agent in charge and in 1992 was appointed as the deputy assistant director in charge of the FBI's New York office. There he oversaw the unprecedented investigation of the 1993 bombing of the World Trade Center. Three years later he led the apprehension team that captured the international terrorist and fugitive Ramzi Yousef in Islamabad, Pakistan.

Following his FBI career, Bill became vice president of U.S. Healthcare and, later, president of U.S. Security Care in Philadelphia. In 2000 Bill was appointed vice president of Guardsmark, one of the world's largest security services corporations, and since 2003 he has been president and CEO of The Gavin Group, which performs consulting services for international corporations and conducted the compliance audits for the Catholic Church in the United States to ensure child protection measures are in place.

Bill has a BS in biology from Boston College and an MS in microbiology from Fordham University. He also attended the John F. Kennedy School of Government at Harvard University and is a member of the National Executive Institute. He was the recipient of the U.S. Presidential Distinguished Rank Award and the U.S. Presidential Meritorious Rank Award. Bill lives in Boston.